HOW TO PICK STOCKS

A KIPLINGER BOOK

HOW TO PICK STOCKS

America's Leading Mutual Fund Managers Tell How They Do It

By Fred W. Frailey

KIPLINGER
TIMES BUSINESS

RANDOM HOUSE

KIPLINGER BOOKS

Published by
The Kiplinger Washington Editors, Inc.
1729 H Street, NW
Washington, D.C. 20006

Library of Congress Cataloging-in-Publication Data

Frailey, Fred W.
  How to pick stocks : America's leading mutual fund managers tell how
they do it / by Fred W. Frailey.
    p. cm.
  "A Kiplinger book."
  Includes index.
  ISBN 0–8129–2826–1
    1. Investments—United States—Handbooks, manuals, etc. 2. Stocks—
United States—Handbooks, manuals, etc. 3. Mutual funds—United
States—Handbooks, manuals, etc.   I. Title.
HG4921.F668   1997
332.63'22—DC21   96-49362
                                                                                CIP

This publication is intended to provide guidance in regard to the subject
matter covered. It is sold with the understanding that the author and
publisher are not herein engaged in rendering legal, accounting, tax or
other professional services. If such services are required, professional
assistance should be sought.

9 8 7 6 5 4 3 2 1
First edition. Printed in the United States of America.
Book designed by S. Laird Jenkins Corp.

Contents

There are plenty of wrong ways to pick stocks. For example, you can buy stocks you hear mentioned at a cocktail party, without investigating them yourself. Or you can buy the recommendations of your stockbroker, without understanding the reason for the recommendations and how the stocks complement others in your portfolio.

There are also smart ways to pick stocks...not a single way, but many different, equally successful approaches to stock selection. This book is a showcase of contrasting methodologies used by some of the best stock pickers in the business.

Their wisdom will be useful not just to investors who manage their own portfolios, making all the stock selections themselves. It is equally valuable for those who rely on investment professionals but who want to understand how the advisers think and to participate in the decisions. Even mutual fund investors, who don't own individual issues directly, can use this book to learn which kind of investment strategy they want to see practiced in the funds they buy.

The fund managers interviewed for this book have one very fundamental trait in common—they're not market timers, trying to guess when the broad markets are about to peak, plateau or bottom out. They don't cash out of hot markets or pour money into depressed markets. In markets high or low, hot or shunned, they look for individual companies that, according to their guidelines, will enjoy strong appreciation regardless of what the rest of the market is doing.

At the Kiplinger organization, we endorse this focus on stocks rather than markets. In the 50 years we have been publishing *Kiplinger's* magazine, we have urged our readers to invest on a regular basis in quality equities, without regard for the level of "the market." As early as 1948, in an article entitled "What a Young Man Should Do With His Money (If Any)," we championed a system that is today called "dollar cost averaging." The hypothetical young man in the article should "not try to time his buying for a rise in the market; only 10%

or 15% of investors can correctly judge their timing." (We probably overstated even that modest percentage of successful market timers.)

The early readers of our magazine were young adults who grew up in the Depression, and they harbored an understandable suspicion of the stock market. They were partial to the safety or guaranteed savings and the steady income of bonds, and if they bought stocks at all—which very few Americans did—they gravitated toward low-volatility issues that paid high dividends.

The *Kiplinger Magazine* (later renamed *Changing Times*, and later still *Kiplinger's Personal Finance Magazine*) confronted this cautiousness head on. Article after article argued the superiority of equities over other classes of assets. "The way to make money is to take some risk, and there are ways of minimizing the risk," we wrote in May of 1949. Your goal as a stock investor, we continued, should be "an average annual return on investment of 6 to 10 percent," compared with the 2% to 3% then earned by passbook savings or 4% to 5% in bonds. (I don't think any of our readers blamed us that our target objective for stocks turned out to be well below the actual average total return of quality equities since 1949.)

In that same article, we wrote that the stock investors shouldn't care about dividends, preferring high-growth companies that paid little or no dividends but reinvested their earnings in future growth. The stocks recommended in that May '49 article included Coca-Cola, DuPont, Sears, General Motors and IBM, which collectively, enjoyed a total return of more than 9,000% over the following five decades.

At the Kiplinger organization, we have always been partial to growth stocks, but we also believe that you shouldn't pay outrageous multiples of earnings for even the most dynamic of high-growth companies. It is possible to apply a "value" screen to a group of growth-stock candidates and improve the odds of price appreciation. Of course, if you're a disciplined dollar cost averager—adding to your positions of favored stocks on a regular basis—you don't have to worry about whether you're paying too much at a particular time. Given the volatility of growth stocks, you'll end up buying low as often as you buy high.

If you're determined to become a smart stock picker, study the masters well. Find a method that makes sense to you, fits your temperament, and suits your investment objectives. And then stick to it, even when your strategy is out of favor for a year or two. In investing, consistency is a virtue. Flitting from one investing style to another is a sure guarantee that the strategy you've just abandoned is the one that's just about to shine.

The mutual fund managers interviewed for this book are the royalty of portfolio management today. But like all royalty, they are also mortal. They have their ups and downs, like all investors. If, after sampling the wisdom of this royalty, you decide that the emperor has no clothes, you can always abandon stock picking altogether. There is always the refuge of unmanaged index funds or throwing darts at the stock listings. You might do just fine, but you won't have nearly as much fun, or learn as much about business, finance and the fascinating companies that are shaping tomorrow's world.

A word about Fred Frailey, deputy editor of *Kiplinger's* magazine who put together this book: The value in these pages comes as much from him as from the money managers who are profiled. Fred selected the managers he deemed worthy of educating you, our reader, and he is a very tough, discerning critic of portfolio management. It is Fred's insightful questions that make his interviews such a joy to read, challenging the managers to lay out their ideas with boldness and clarity.

I hope you find this a useful addition to your stock-picking education. Effective investing is a process of continuous self-education, and there's no substitute for trial and error. May your trials be not too grueling, and may your successes outnumber your errors.

Knight Kiplinger

Editor in Chief, *Kiplinger's Personal Finance Magazine*
February 1997

Part I

Learn from the Pros

O n the face of it, this book is about how two dozen men and women created billions of dollars of wealth for shareholders of their mutual funds in the 1990s—their methods and techniques, the rules they live and die by, and even how they console themselves when their methods don't work or when they make mistakes—all from the horse's mouth, in their own words. In that sense, it's an investment textbook straight from the trading desk, and hopefully, more interesting to read than any you've seen before.

Sure, funds managers are investing millions—other people's money no less—and chances are, you're not. But, like you, fund managers have to decide what and when to buy and sell. They aim to meet their fund's objectives, producing the best possible return given the types of assets the fund owns, its guiding philosophy and its tolerance for risk. They develop an investing strategy. And, when the market calls for it, successful fund managers, as the interviews will show, adjust their tactics while sticking to their strategies.

Whatever your choice of investments—individual stocks or mutual funds—this anthology will help you develop, reaffirm or revise your investing goals and your strategies for achieving them. I'm quite confident that you'll come away from this book with insights that will make you a better investor.

What Makes Them the Pros

At *Kiplinger's Personal Finance Magazine* we talk to hundreds of professional money managers and nonprofessional individual investors over the course of a year. And we understand why the pros so often do better than the rest of us in buying and selling securities:

Direction.

The best ones have a systematic approach to stock (or bond) picking. The rest of us flit from rosebud to rosebud.

Grit.

They don't deviate from their approach when results aren't forthcoming. The rest of us might cut and run.

Staying power.

They invest for the long term. We lack patience.

Moxie.

They don't try to predict the unknowable—such as what the markets will do next. We do.

Focus.

They stay focused, filtering out extraneous advice and information. We act on whatever we hear last.

Those common links separate the pros from the rest of us mere mortals. Still, if there's anything you'll quickly learn from *How to Pick Stocks,* it's that there is no single way for everyone to make money as an investor. There are as many ways as there are successful investors. Each of the portfolio managers profiled in this book goes about the task of investing differently. This is, of course, both a curse and a blessing to the rest of us. It's a curse because it means there are no magic incantations to memorize; it really is our own responsibility as investors to figure out what each of us can do comfortably and successfully to make our own money grow. And it's a blessing because the diversity of approaches described within these covers is proof, if you needed it, that any number of well-thought-out and faithfully executed investment techniques can yield great results over time, and that you don't need to be a genius, after all.

One thing that comes to me again and again upon reading these chapters is that these people are making money even when they invest in direct contradiction to each other's techniques. I mean, how easy can it get? Foster Friess of Brandywine fund gets new ideas looking at the list of stocks setting new highs. "What's the appeal of a stock hitting new lows?" he asks. Foster thinks that a cheap stock is probably a dog. But John Neff spent a professional lifetime at Vanguard Windsor fund profitably pursuing those "woebegone, misunderstood and overlooked" stocks inhabiting the new-lows list.

That these two people could go in different directions and end up at the same place, in the chips, shouldn't surprise you. The stock market is not a zero-sum game. Over time prices always go up. Moreover, whereas Friess likes stocks that are going up and Neff is happy buying ones going down—perhaps they've even been on the opposite side of the same trades some days—each does so in the context of an overall plan that he has confidence in and stick to. Robert Sanborn, who founded Oakmark fund explains it this way: "The one unpardonable thing an investment person can do is to abandon his discipline— the investment methods. I was watching the [Chicago] Bulls last night. This is a great team. But they lost—Denver had them by 30 points. And it was interesting. The Bulls didn't exactly panic, but they veered away from the playing style that has worked well for them. The same thing can happen in the investment business. After two or three bad years, people can question their style and start surfing from one philosophy to another. Please shoot me if I ever do that."

Often these professionals are doing practically the same thing, with variations. For instance, Mario Gabelli, of the Gabelli family of funds, and Oakmark's Sanborn both buy the same sort of stock: one selling at a significant discount to its private market value, that is, what a rational investor would pay to buy the whole company. But whereas Gabelli also prefers stocks faithful to an investment theme (which in his case might mean a company active in multimedia businesses) and wants a catalyst that will cause his stocks to rise, Sanborn places his special emphasis on companies whose managers are already committed to raising the share price over time.

Or take Brandywine and Twentieth Century Ultra. Each buys

stocks whose earnings and share price are both rocketing up, and each strives to be buying just as soon as these trends become apparent. But whereas Ultra's managers pay no attention to price-earnings ratios and other signposts of value, and don't have much contact with the companies whose shares they own, Brandywine's people don't like to overpay, and they stay in frequent touch with the companies. Which subset of this momentum style is better? It depends. Ultra has slightly better five- and ten-year returns, but it is noticeably more volatile.

Why This Book?

The genesis of *How to Pick Stocks* was an idea from *Kiplinger's* reader Fred Zimmerman, of Chapel Hill, N.C. Fred suggested that we publish a series of Q&A pieces with fund managers, but not the kind you usually see, in which the manager prattles off a list of stocks that he or she likes and why. Instead, he wanted to know *how* they went about their jobs of investing his money. (At the time, Fred owned shares of 18 funds.) "And be sure to ask," he added, "how they felt when nothing they did worked, and even their dog thought they were stupid." Great idea! I wish I'd thought of it first. Ted Miller, the editor of *Kiplinger's Personal Finance Magazine,* embraced the notion, too, and off I went, usually with my colleague Manuel Schiffres, the magazine's senior investment writer.

The first "Insider Interview" appeared in *Kiplinger's* August 1992 issue, with Kenneth Heebner, the manager of CGM Capital Development. I thought then that this series, appearing roughly every other month, would become repetitive after a year or so and die a natural death.

Well, more than four years and two dozen "Insider Interviews" later, the show continues, and I think the reason is simply this: When people who love their jobs talk about their work, the words come easy, like electric current through a wire. There are countless ways for investors to make money in stocks. I never grow tired of hearing them, and hope I never do.

Investing is not a "game." It's not rigged, except against those who don't do the necessary work but resort to shortcuts. And it's not boring—certainly not to me or to the subjects of these interviews. Gosh, they do like to talk.

The interviews appear here pretty much as they did originally, because the topic of picking stocks is really timeless. I omitted a small amount of material that was plainly dated, and in several instances added some other dialogue that, in retrospect, I wish had appeared the first time around. And I spoke again with each of the interviewees, to bring you up to date with some of the things discussed in the original pieces. A couple of "Insider Interviews" are omitted because the specialties of the interviewees (quantitative analysis, technical analysis and investment newsletter performance) are outside the ken of most individual investors. Four of these interviews first appeared in the magazine's sister publication, *Kiplinger's Mutual Funds,* which is published annually. And in one instance, so much had happened to the fund and its manager (Rod Linafelter of Berger One Hundred) that the sensible thing was to go back to Denver and redo the whole thing, which we did.

The fact that many of these interviews took place over several years will provide you with added perspective on investing. You'll see what the manager said and did at the time of the original interview, the outcome, and why he or she thought the fund performed that way. Some did great, some not so great. But none of the managers abandoned their fundamental belief in their approach and changed course. They may have adapted to conditions as they found them, but that's all.

Before You Meet the Managers

If you buy and sell individual stocks, be alert for fund managers whose investment styles resemble your own. Or if you're a style surfer not yet certain about which investment method to adopt, look for those that intuitively make the most sense to you. In either case, ask yourself:

- What are these people doing that I'm not? Or,

- What do they do better?

You don't have to be a stock picker to benefit from *How to Pick Stocks*. It frightens me sometimes how little many investors know about the mutual funds in which they invest. That's the same as buying a stock without a reason for owning it. Knowing how a manager invests your money will make you a smarter shareholder. You'll know why the fund behaves the way it does most times. And you will possess the information you need to diversify your fund holdings across a spectrum of investment styles—larger companies, smaller companies, those with fast earnings growth or those with low valuations—that you'll find represented by the managers we interviewed. Find a manager whose philosophy you admire and whose style of fund meets your portfolio's needs and you can invest in that manager's fund (if it's open to new investors) or find another one that reflects a similar philosophy.

After you've read all the interviews and gleaned the many ideas presented there, the last chapter will help you formulate—or reformulate—your personal investing strategy.

The Value Investors

Mario Gabelli

Mark Mobius

John Neff

Michael Price

Robert Sanborn

Kent Simons & Larry Marx

Roland Whitridge

Vague labels like "growth" and "value" are things we journalists lean on like a crutch to make arbitrary distinctions between money managers. Sometimes the labels are apt, sometimes not. Donald Yacktman considers himself a "value" investor, but Yacktman's fund is crammed with steadily growing companies, and it's in the growth section of this book that you'll find him (page 165). By the same token, Ralph Wanger doesn't consider Acorn to be a growth fund, and true enough, it exhibits characteristics of both a growth and a value portfolio. But because Acorn is more growth than value, he, too, will be found with the growth crowd (page 156). And while Jerome Dodson invests with an eye toward value and stocks with strong earnings growth, he and his socially conscious Parnassus fund resist either label; you'll find him in Part 4, "Switch Hitters & Niche Hitters," beginning on page 184.

But of the fund managers interviewed in this section, you can be by-god certain that they are value investors, and proud of it. Listen to Mario Gabelli or Mark Mobius or Robert Sanborn for a while and you begin to think they got their old-time value religion straight from a pulpit, delivered to them by an unrelenting voice. To hear them tell it, to invest any other way is blasphemy.

Stated most simply, value investors are bargain hunters. They don't buy a stock because its earnings are going up. True, the earnings sometimes *are* going up, maybe rapidly, but that's immaterial to the value investor's stock-selection process. What's really important is that by some measure the stock be cheap in relation to what its price ought to be—maybe cheap compared with its earnings now and in the future. One common yardstick for this— the one published every day in every big-city newspaper for practically every stock—is the *price-earnings ratio (or P/E)*. That's arrived at by dividing the price per share by earnings per share.

Professional investors rarely rely on the newspaper version of the P/E ratio, which reflects earnings of the previous 12 months—what has already happened. The stock market anticipates events as much as it reacts to them, so an army of analysts is constantly at work calculating what the earnings of companies *may* be in the future, such as for the current year, next year and even the next five years. Those estimates are continually being refined and adjusted and collected and averaged and massaged in more ways than you can imagine. Most times they're wrong. The people in these pages don't pay that much attention to P/E ratios, anyway. Estimates are too imprecise, subject to too much manipulation by cunning managements, and buffeted by too many special one-time additions and subtractions.

Another yardstick: *price–book value ratio*. It used to be said that a stock trading for less than its book value per share—its total assets minus its total liabilities—was undervalued. But if the meaning of P/E ratios has been distorted by the corporate machinations of the 1980s and 1990s, the P/B ratio has simply been destroyed by writeoffs and the like. Robert Sanborn puts it best: "Book value has little or no relation to real value. Philip Morris values its Marlboro brand name at zero, and it's the most valuable asset the company has. When I joined Harris Associates, one of the oldest senior partners was managing some private money and bought only below-book-value stocks. Within a month this guy hated my guts because I was always lobbying him to get rid of that criterion and to broaden his investment philosophy. There's no intuitiveness to it. As the market went up, it became virtually impossible for him to find stocks that met his criteria. He capitulated. I generally work on people long enough until they give in, just to get rid of me."

John Neff's definition of a value stock is simple: any stock that's "woebegone, misunderstood and overlooked," But that doesn't help you much, does it? Sometimes, he says, the undervalued stock is one that is down somewhat from its high price, for no particular reason having to do with its own business. Or he might be referring to a cyclical stock, such as a metals company, whose price is down because its profits are down because demand for its products is weak. Neff will calculate what this metals company might earn if demand rose in a more robust economy, and declare this stock seriously undervalued. Or he may simply be attracted to a stock that's undervalued for good reasons but about to undergo a change in its fortunes for the better.

Mario Gabelli keys off a variation of the P/E ratio in deciding what's undervalued. He calls it EBITD—that is, earnings before interest, taxes and depreciation, minus the capital spending needed to maintain the business. This is more useful to Gabelli than just earnings because some of the media stocks he buys, such as cable-TV providers, don't have any earnings. But they do have a lot of positive cash flow, and that's what EBITD tries to capture.

Michael Price likes to establish values by taking a company apart mentally, asking what each piece would be worth on its own, then adding up the numbers. Or he asks what might happen to the share price if an imaginative CEO came in and tightened up a loosely run company—spun off this part, sold that part, closed down one operation and expanded another.

Out on the edges of the earth, emerging-markets investor Mark

Mobius likes "to buy stocks whose prices are going down, not up." Because his venue is just about any developing country in the world, he sometimes measures the *comparative value* of stocks in the same industry in several countries, and after adjusting for accounting differences, goes with the ones that are least expensive based on their earnings or cash flow. "But we never come up with absolute answers," he confesses.

And Sanborn, in company even with some folks whom I would call growth investors, defines value as a price that's significantly below what a deep-pockets dude from Texas would pay to buy the whole company and convert it to a private business. (Gabelli also calculates such private market values, and so does Yacktman.)

But enough of this. Let's let these people speak for themselves.

Mario Gabelli

There's a Mario Gabelli fund for every taste—a dozen so far, with Gabelli managing or supervising seven of them. Gabelli Asset is a down-the-middle fund that looks for undervalued companies. Gabelli Value takes huge positions in a few undervalued stocks. There are funds for ultraconservative investors (Gabelli ABC), small-company lovers (Gabelli Small Cap Growth), entertainment and media aficionados (Gabelli Global Interactive Couch Potato), sector players (Gabelli Global Telecommunications), gold bugs (Gabelli Gold), closed-end-fund investors (Gabelli Equity Trust and Gabelli Global Multimedia Trust) and even a fund for growth investors (Gabelli Growth).

You can't argue with results, either. From its start in 1986 through late 1996, Gabelli Asset handily beat the overall stock market. So did Gabelli Growth, begun in 1987. Gabelli Value, his third-largest fund, is more concentrated and volatile. The Asset and Value funds are outstanding performers in years when undervalued stocks are in the limelight, and Growth has done best when stocks with strong earnings growth held investor attention.

Of course, you're entitled to ask whether this man is stretched too thin. Are there limits even to Super Mario? That question was on the agenda when we spoke with Gabelli, born in 1943, at his offices in Rye, New York, late in 1994.

KIPLINGER'S: You practice value investing a bit differently than most other money managers who go after undervalued stocks. What's your approach?

GABELLI: Value investing, the way I define it, is finding a good business run by smart people at a reasonably good price relative to its values today and five or more years from now.

When I started this firm in 1977, you couldn't figure out what a company's tax rate was or what its real earnings were because inflation had accelerated and made depreciation numbers hard to analyze. So I said, "Look, it's very simple: If you were an informed industrialist or a very wealthy person, what would you pay for the entire company? And what will that company be worth in five, ten or 15 years?"

And how do you go about answering those questions?

The same way we always have, by focusing on EBITD—that is, earnings before interest, taxes and depreciation, minus the capital spending needed to maintain the business. That's easy. Anybody coming out of business school can do it. The hard part is to know what multiple of EBITD to pay for that company. Once you know that, you can calculate its value five to 15 years out. I call this range of future prices the "private market value channel," and when the stock market knocks a stock well below that channel, I get excited.

Will you wait indefinitely for the stock market to come to love your undervalued stocks?

The ideal stock comes with a catalyst—something that will bring the public to it. For instance, in the case of American Express, it's a lot of little things: Harvey Golub succeeding James Robinson and "skinnying down" the business—spinning off Lehman Brothers, focusing on the basic green-card business, buying back stock. Each of these things helped bring the stock back.

Does every stock you own have to have a catalyst or else you don't buy?

Sometimes we buy things that involve old-fashioned judgment. Another kind of ideal stock would be a company selling at a low price-earnings multiple with no debt and sound management that's sensitive to growing the value of the company. Pittway, for instance, fits this description. It has rising earnings because of rising revenues, and it has a rising P/E multiple, too.

You're talking like a growth-stock investor now.

But we were able to buy 30% of Pittway when nobody else wanted it—the stock kept going down or sideways. You can find these things if you just look hard enough. For instance, I go to the burglar-alarm show in New York. Three years ago there was nobody there from Wall Street. Last year there were three analysts to look over the participating companies, this year four.

It's true you own a lot of stocks that nobody's ever heard of.

Well, stepping back, what do we stand for? We've always done the same thing: bottom-up stock picking. We go with domestic stocks, mostly, although that's changing. We're value-oriented. We're both small-capitalization and big-cap—we don't care about a company's size.

At how large a discount to private market value are you looking to buy?

I don't do it that way. I start off asking: How much money should we make? Our goal is to achieve absolute results. I want to earn 10% a year after taxes and inflation. To do that I need to pick stocks that will go up 25% a year. If I can pick one that does this for two years and pay the long-term capital-gains tax, which is now 28%, I'll be left with a two-year gain of 36%. If inflation runs at 3% or 4%, that leaves me with maybe a 30% gain—13% to 14% annualized. If I make enough mistakes with other stocks, that gain comes down to about a 10% real return for the funds as a whole. Our low turnover helps, so you can defer paying taxes.

The ideal candidate is a stock like Media General, which you can buy for $30 but is really worth $80, and whose value keeps growing faster than inflation. Even if the stock is $75 two years from now, it will still be a bargain—a great example of a company whose big cable-TV franchise I can get for free.

For free? How so?

In a multifaceted company such as Media General, you look at each of the pieces. Media General has newspapers in Tampa,

Richmond and Winston-Salem, N.C. You calculate their revenues and EBITDs. You ask about their circulations and the prices these circulations would command if the newspapers were sold. In other words, what is the value of the newspaper franchise now, and what will it be in five years?

Then you look at Media General's TV stations, in Tampa and Jacksonville, Fla. The company also has two newsprint plants, an off-balance-sheet interest in a partnership that owns the Denver Post and, finally, its 220,000 cable-TV subscribers.

You add all these numbers up. And if Media General were to sell those 220,000 cable subscribers for $650 million, you'd still be left with a company worth much more than its current price. So when I say that I am giving you the cable subscribers for free, I've done the math and am hyping the result for the purpose of discussion.

How much of Media General do you own?

About 30% of the company. The Bryant family that runs Media General really doesn't own anything. But they have all the votes; there are two classes of shares.

Could you take us through the process you used in deciding to buy a stock recently?

Hilton hotels is a good example. Hilton dropped to $50 in June of 1994 from a high of $75. There are 50 million shares, so the market capitalization of the company is roughly $2.5 billion. Hilton has two businesses. One is hotels, under the Hilton brand name in the U.S. and the Conrad's name overseas, because they had sold the Hilton name overseas to someone else. And the other business is gambling.

We saw what others saw—namely, that the gaming business was going national and international, and that within that framework Hilton has some very valuable assets: a good brand name, an A rating on its balance sheet and a chairman approaching age 70, with a big block of stock, who is committed to selling the company.

So when we did the analysis of the hotel properties, we came up with a value equal to the entire price of the stock, because with fewer hotels being built and demand rising, the properties are more profitable and are worth more.

Then we analyzed the global gaming business and felt that the company split into those two pieces would be worth at least the $90 it would take to give us the rate of return we needed. We already owned some, but now we've bought more. When it got to $70 we didn't sell, and I think that at $62, where it closed last night, we can make another 50% by late 1996.

In addition to evaluating stocks by their private market value, you also superimpose investment themes, don't you?

I started my career as a broadcast analyst, and I own some TV stations personally. I think we have one of the best analytical grasps of the telephone, media and entertainment stocks. We're very good at analyzing the movie business and prerecorded music, and very good at cable television.

Let's talk about the Gabelli funds. What distinguishes Asset from Value besides the fact that Value is sold through brokers?

Gabelli Asset's holdings are clustered into three categories: one-third industrial stocks, one-third consumer stocks and one-third media stocks. It's a down-the-middle fund.

Whereas Gabelli Value will put one-third of assets in a single stock . . .

Value fund, at its launch, was meant to make big investments in stocks we really like. That's why it had an inordinate amount of Paramount stock—30% of assets when it was bought out.

In terms of assets, Value is a shadow of its former self. Why did investors bail out?

It was designed as a fund for Shearson brokers to sell. Then a lot of Shearson brokers resigned to go with other firms, and when they did they sold my fund—I had a lot of redemptions. It was my first load fund. We're pretty good investment managers, but we're not great at marketing. So we had the Shearson organization do this deal.

Have you considered converting Gabelli Value to no-load?
No.

But wasn't Shearson a fair-weather friend?
That's unfair. Shearson continues to be one of the finest retail organizations as part of Smith Barney. It continues to nurture the fund. But it's not pounding the table selling its shares, and I've not been down there demanding a new sales drive.

You started a bunch of new funds the past year. Why?
We made the decision to have a series of funds with global reach. The first was Gabelli Global Telecommunications, with my telephone analyst, Sal Muoio, running it. Then in February of this year came Gabelli Global Interactive Couch Potato fund, which has me, Sal, my son Mark Gabelli and Ivan Artega all working on it. This fund follows the media-distribution companies—cable, broadcasting, newspapers, and so on. We want to keep it 60% domestic stocks, 40% foreign stocks.

Gabelli Global Convertible Securities fund is run by Hart Woodson. Very few people like to concentrate on convertibles, but Hart is 35 years old and has been analyzing them for years. The fourth fund is Gabelli Gold, with Caesar Bryan. Caesar was with the Lexington funds, but Lexington wasn't willing to do what I do.

And that is . . .
Create personalities. I did it with Elizabeth Bramwell. We believe in personalities. We believe the investor should understand who runs the fund. Of course, it isn't good for the management company when, like Elizabeth, the manager leaves to start a new fund.

So to market the funds, you market yourself?
Yes. I'm not sure that's good or bad. I don't like it. Ned Johnson [chairman of Fidelity Investments] stays in the woodwork and brings

out the stars. What I want to do is find more people like Elizabeth. I'm creating a Caesar Bryan, a Sal Muoio, a Hart Woodson. I want ten or 15 individuals who are great personalities and known for their niche.

But Mario, a lot of these funds show you as the manager. This came to us from a reader who owns Gabelli Asset: "Gabelli keeps opening new funds and managing them himself and won't close funds when they get huge. You can't tell me he can find that many values. He's got way too much on his plate, and that bothers me." Are you overextended?

We haven't done a good job of conveying the fact that all Gabelli funds aren't run by Gabelli. And there's an economic fact of life: If I want to hire a very good equity-income manager, it will cost me half a million dollars. A new fund with $20 million in assets and a 1% management fee would lose $300,000 just on that basis. I grew up in the Bronx, and when I started this company 17 years ago, I couldn't raise $100,000. So, yeah, if somebody looks at me today and says, "You made a lot of money," it wasn't always that way. I still ride subways! So I'm not going to go out and load down a small fund with an expensive manager. I would rather incubate it myself and then turn it over to somebody to run.

Are you looking to replace yourself on any of the funds right now?

I'd like to hire somebody to run Gabelli Small Cap fund, and I have an active search on for someone to take over Gabelli Growth. A money manager is harder to find than someone to run the business side of an investment company. There are very few people around who do bottom-up research and know their companies. Plenty of people run their computers and devise income models for companies, but that's not our culture.

Plus, you run the firm . . .

Yes, and I don't like it. I'm an analyst and money manager. I had a guy come in to run the business about ten years ago. He had a tax background and he annoyed an IRS agent, which sparked a personal vendetta against the firm. In 1984, when we had only $3 million in capital, a government agency was saying we had too much capital. I'm looking for someone to manage the firm for me again. But to go back to whether we're spread too thin . . .

Yes.

We did close Gabelli Global Convertible Securities because we didn't find values. And in Gabelli Asset, if we don't find values we like, we don't aggressively buy things. So I don't subscribe to the argument that we're spread too thin. I'm doing the same amount of research today as I did in 1968, when I was at Loeb Rhoades. That's half my time. I used to use the other half to write research reports. Now I write quarterly letters and look for people to hire.

Going into 1996, Mario Gabelli hadn't made a lot of progress in the hiring department. In fact, he lost his star telecommunications stock picker, Sal Muoio, to Lazard Frères. But the boss took it in stride. "Now we pay him commissions to get his ideas," said Gabelli, "as opposed to paying him a salary, as we did before." But he did replace himself at the helm of Gabelli Growth, hiring Howard Ward, formerly of Scudder, Stevens & Clark, and immediately began featuring Ward in ads. Behold, an investment personality was being born.

The year 1995 was made to order for stocks fueled by rapid earnings growth—precisely what almost none of the Gabelli funds look to buy. Given that fact, the flagship Asset and Value funds did okay, but not spectacularly, producing returns of almost 30%. His funds still held their investments in Media General, Hilton and Pittway. In March of 1996, Mario Gabelli could say: "The stocks that were dull last year are good this year. Hilton was down 8% in 1995, but is up 50% in just two months of 1996. So patience pays."

Media General, after only an 8% rise (including dividends) in 1995, was up smartly in 1996, too. I asked Gabelli if he perhaps erred with Media General by buying so heavily into a company in which his shares had no voting power. After all, why should the Bryant family at Media General listen to this pesky fund manager who owns one-third of their company? "Nobody listens to anybody," he replied. "Yesterday our brokerage affiliate hosted a meeting for a company called Greif Brothers. Greif Brothers was created 119 years ago, and went public in 1926. They had not had a meeting with shareholders in 70 years—yesterday was the first. That's one end of the spectrum. Media General is somewhat shy of that benchmark."

The landmark telecommunications legislation enacted early in 1996 promises to keep Gabelli busy the rest of this decade: Deregulation of the broadcasting and cable and telephone industries is right up his alley of expertise, and Gabelli thought it would also entwine Media General. "I think what's going to happen is that a company like Southwestern Bell, which has a cable system of its own, is going to knock on Media General's door and suggest they put their systems together and create a new public company." And if so, Mario Gabelli's ship will have come in, again.

Mark Mobius

L ives there an investor who wouldn't envy Mark Mobius his job? There he is, touring a rubber plantation in Thailand or a bicycle factory in China . . . motoring through Turkey . . . talking to businessmen in India . . . inspecting a factory in Brazil . . . or taking a breather in London. Mobius, in case you haven't heard, is Sir John Templeton's subaltern in what used to be called the Third World. More than anyone else, Mobius gave emerging markets a good name.

In February 1987, Mobius launched Templeton Emerging Markets, a closed-end fund traded on the New York Stock Exchange and the first publicly listed U.S. fund to focus specifically on stocks in the world's developing countries. At the time, the idea of targeting a fund solely to the smallest, least developed and most volatile markets in the world may have seemed bizarre—doubly so because Mobius was fixated on undervalued stocks when the supposed allure of these economies was the rapid growth of their companies. And that first year, the year of the crash, Templeton Emerging Markets' total return on assets was −15%. But its portfolio went another seven years without a down year. In 1993 its total return on net asset value was a stunning 97%.

In 1991, Mobius began Templeton Developing Markets, an open-end fund sold through brokers with a 5.75% sales charge. The fund returned 74.5% in '93—its best performance so far.

Mobius, born in 1936 (the Year of the Rat in China, he notes) to a German father and American mother, is today a German citizen. He works out of Hong Kong. But because he likes to see what he's investing in, he is usually somewhere else. I first interviewed him in Washington, D.C., in mid 1994.

KIPLINGER'S: A lot is being said now about the dangers of investing in emerging markets. Do you share that concern?

MOBIUS: Yes. In America, we think democracy is like air—you breathe it and it's free. But you don't have pluralistic societies or democracies everywhere. Transitions from one government to another are painful and sometimes violent, even in the Philippines, which I consider one of the most politically developed countries in Asia.

On another level, our funds constantly place orders to buy and sell in these stock markets, and others notice it. There's not the protection you have in America against insider trading or front-running by brokers. In the emerging markets, these practices are standard operating procedure.

There's a perception that billions of Yankee dollars were thrown into these illiquid markets, causing stock prices to skyrocket last year. Do you buy that argument?

Yes, occasionally we will stimulate a market. But foreigners don't really move markets. Domestic investors in these countries move the markets. Unfortunately, they act on the basis of rumor, trends, outlook and emotion.

But one side of the argument is absolutely correct. Our emerging-markets funds went last year from a little more than $1 billion in assets to $5 billion. The avalanche of money helped send prices up.

Last year was spectacularly successful for all the emerging-markets funds. Did that increase the chances of a blowoff?

It increased both the dangers and the opportunities. You must remember the evolution of these emerging markets. When we started Templeton Emerging Markets in 1987, there were only five markets we could invest in—Hong Kong, Malaysia, the Philippines, Singapore and Thailand. Hong Kong was the pivot, and you know what happened during the crash: The head of the Hong Kong Stock Exchange closed it for a week, and when it reopened we had lost 30%. Others did far worse. That's what I mean by danger.

The opportunity is for those who have the discipline to say, "No, I will be patient because this money is attracting a lot of flies." Right now, we're 30% in cash in the open-end fund and 15% cash in the closed-end fund.

Too many people look at the short term and, when they give you money, want you to be fully invested at once. That was the case in 1987. All the clients were saying, "Get invested! Get invested! The markets are going up!" And of course, being value investors we took our sweet time. We saw these markets rising and said to ourselves, "Now, wait a minute. Unless profits are skyrocketing, the values are decreasing." So we arrived in October of '87 with 30% of assets in cash. When the Hong Kong market reopened after being closed for a week, we had a field day, because brokers desperate to unload stocks were calling us with tremendous offers. They'd say, "Ten-fifty!" And I'd reply, "Nine-twenty!" and they'd say, "Done!" That provided a tremendous platform for us.

Again, early this year many of the emerging stock markets in the Pacific region tanked. But your funds were hurt less than most. What happened?

We were not heavy in Asia at that time, and we had a very high cash position. This was a beautiful example of diversification. You're much better off with a broad global fund than one that is invested exclusively in one emerging market. If I'm doing a single-country fund, my criteria have to be lower because I don't have the number of choices that a global investor has.

Where do you get your ideas for stocks?

We start by gathering information on all the stocks in every one of the 24 nations in which we can invest. We put it all into the computer. There are thousands of companies in that data base.

All of it speaking to you in a Babel of tongues. Where does the data come from?

We get stuff from the stock exchanges and from the companies themselves. We also have consultants in all these countries who gather annual reports, stock-exchange data and so forth for us.

Our first order of business is to learn the accounting systems in each of these countries.

If they have one . . .

Yes, but the accounting systems are very much in place in most countries. The problem is, each country's culture, legal system and society influence how it does accounting. Koreans, being so strict on themselves, have a very, very detailed accounting system, as do the Japanese—the itemizations drive you crazy because they don't group things. In South America, they have a very sophisticated accounting system because they have to account for inflation by updating asset values.

So you learn the accounting systems, and your scouts send material in by the bushel. Then what?

Then our analysts sift this information and try to arrive at some comparative values between countries. This leads to a lot of adjustments. For example, say you want to compare an American company with a Brazilian company. The valuation in America is book value, which is often understated because it is set at original cost, which may have been ten years ago. In Brazil, because of inflation, they revalue constantly; otherwise, the numbers would be meaningless. Another example: depreciation policies. One country, because of government regulation, may not allow accelerated depreciation, so that tax revenue will stay high. Or there may be depreciation differences between industries. Depreciation policy can turn a profit into a loss very quickly. So we have to look at real earnings and cash flow. But we never come up with absolute answers.

As a value investor, what do you look for?

I like to buy stocks whose prices are going down, not up. Can I tell you a story? The Japanese gave us money to run an Indonesian fund in 1991, at what turned out to be the peak of the Indonesian market. I remember once asking a Japanese fund manager how he

picked stocks. He said, "I select stocks that are going up." Period. It
was a great method if your market constantly goes up, which Japan's
did. Anyway, we started looking at the numbers in the Indonesian
market when we got this money and thought—these are the comparisons we always make—that relative to the companies' history, the
market was expensive; relative to other markets in the region, it was
expensive; and relative to similar industries around the world, it was
expensive. What to do? Our investors said, "Hurry! Get 100% invested
now. Otherwise, you're not earning your fee." But it took us a year
and a half just to get 80% invested.

Did they ever thank you for saving their skins?
Now they do. But then we were having a hell of a time. First,
when prices were rising, they wanted me to buy. Then when the
market fell, they didn't want me to keep buying because they were
losing money. The problem is that people don't have a long time
frame. When a stock market is down 20%, a value-oriented manager is
probably buying.

**You haven't mentioned government stability. Do you take
that into account in making investment decisions?**
I look at that, but through the eyes and ears of the managers of
the companies in which I invest. I will go into a country and ask a
manager what is happening to that industry—whether there are
price controls or subsidies or import duties. I ask what the
government is likely to do to that company this year or next. They
will tell you what they fear.

**Do you ever make calls on entire stock markets—decide
Turkey or China is the place to be in the next year and load up?**
No.

**Then why is your fund stuffed at present with stocks from
Turkey and Brazil?**
I found the most buys there. It's easy to talk about the markets of

individual countries. But when you get down to how we invest, we don't think that way. We say, "Where are the bargains?"

Do you visit a company before you buy its stock—check out those rubber trees, so to speak?

Ninety percent of the time we see the management before buying. Every once in a while the numbers may look so tempting on a stock that we begin nibbling at its shares. But we won't load up until we've seen the company.

How do you communicate with companies across all the language barriers?

Besides English, I speak a smattering of five languages. But I don't use them to ask difficult questions. Most businesspeople around the world speak English or will have a translator available.

Can you describe how you came to buy a typical stock in your portfolios?

Cukurova Elektrik, a hydroelectric utility in Turkey, was privatized by the government, and then the controlling interest was bought by another private group. This caused a stir in the market because a lot of people thought this group would use the utility as a cash cow. We accepted the bet and went to take a look. I remember that it took seven bone-jarring hours in a truck to get to the plant in the south of Turkey.

So much for the glamorous life of an emerging-markets investor.

Quite. Actually, I'd been there previously, when the government owned it, and was impressed by its efficiency. This time, as before, they could answer all the questions and provide statistics. The rate structure was favorable. They were expanding by building new transmission lines. The balance sheet was very sound. In the end, we decided that the group that bought the controlling interest would do well by it and bought shares, too.

We make a lot of comparisons across nations. If there's a hydro-electric plant in Turkey, we find similar ones in other countries and look at the values. There should be no significant disparity, provided that electricity rates are not that different from country to country.

When we bought shares of Cukurova Elektrik, its price-earnings ratio was 6, and the price-to-book-value ratio was 60%. We found electric companies elsewhere selling at P/Es of 12 to 15 and at a premium to book value.

All this happened in 1989, and we still own the stock.

What convinces you to sell a stock?

When we find something cheaper. That's the theory. In reality, what happens is that you sell something to buy that cheap stock, and when you arrive with cash in hand, it's not there at the price you thought you could get it for. That's why, as value investors, it's almost a given that we'll have lots of cash, even though we don't plan it that way.

Do you set price targets for stocks you buy?

Definitely. There's no good reason to buy unless you can double your money.

Over how long?

However long it takes. Waiting doesn't bother me.

But when your methods are totally out of favor, aren't you sometimes tempted to change those methods?

Of course I'm tempted. I was once a technical analyst. I followed the charts. They were good for the macro picture. I was able to predict some movements of the markets. But the charts were not a good way of investing, because even if you could predict that the market would go up or down, when it came to specific stocks the chart system didn't work as well. Anyway, we are constantly testing other ways of investing.

Such as?

Such as momentum investing—buying stocks because they are going up in price. This didn't work as well as the value system we use. But one of the things I believe in is not to be rigid in the methods I use. I can't dig a hole and put my head in it. I've got to be willing to find out what's happening around me and to be flexible. But at the same time I must make decisions based on facts, and the fact is that, historically, value investing works. And unless it is proven otherwise, I'm not going to change.

As you travel, what forces do you see at work that will affect the developing countries in which you invest?

One, there's more food than ever before, and that means healthier people. Two, better medicines and better health care are extending lives, and longer life spans mean more opportunities for education and experience, and so literacy rates go up. Then add trends in mass communication. There are 96 million television sets in China. As a percentage of all Chinese households, that's a small number. But the impact on the lives of people is tremendous. People sitting in China can look at *Dallas* and wonder why they are not living the way the Americans do. They see a kitchen on TV the size of their whole house. They want the same thing, and they want it now.

Politicians can't run from this anymore. They've got to come up with answers. Communism doesn't work. Socialism doesn't work. Peronism doesn't work. Market economies work. Why? Because they utilize natural human behavior.

Your closed-end fund, Templeton Emerging Markets, has at times traded at a 17% premium to net-asset value. Would you be a buyer of its shares yourself?

If the premium is more than 10%, no. I'd buy Templeton Developing Markets, the open-end fund. It has a 5.75% load but the same portfolio.

What portion of an investor's portfolio should be invested in emerging markets?

Anyone over the age of 40 should limit this kind of investment to 10% of his or her portfolio. But if you are younger, then perhaps you can afford to invest more because your time horizon is longer. I've had clients put their babies' money in the funds. It's a tremendous burden on my head.

Now that you've mentioned your head, it's fair to ask about the trademark of your distinctive appearance. Are you totally bald?

I decided a long time ago that for the little bit of hair that was there, it was more convenient to shave it than to go to a barber shop to snip a little bit around the edges.

The next two years confirmed my respect for Mark Mobius. The total returns of his funds weren't stupendous, because developing markets almost everywhere went to sleep in 1994 and 1995. But in that difficult environment, Mobius, with his nose to the ground, concentrating on valuations rather than growth rates and on individual companies rather than entire markets, acquitted himself wonderfully. In 1993 he proved with that 75% return what his approach to investing could deliver with the wind to his back. Then in the rather mediocre investment climate in emerging markets of 1994 through 1996 he came through each year with above-average results among the burgeoning ranks of emerging-market funds.

By 1996, the number of Templeton emerging-market funds registered for sale in the U.S. or in other countries, plus private portfolios—all under the control of Mobius—had risen to 32, with assets totaling $8 billion ($2.5 billion of it in Templeton Developing Markets). When I spoke to Mobius again in preparing this book, I asked to what degree he still personally selected the stocks. The answer was that his job is now *not* to pick the stocks, but rather to direct and inspire and backstop the people in each country who actually make the selections. "You must remember we have an organization of more than 40 people who help me find bargains and comb these markets," he said. "The system we use is rather unique, in that every one of them is a portfolio manager in the sense that the bargains they select are going into all of these funds and portfolios. They are organized by country. For instance, we have a guy on South Africa who covers African markets. What happens is that these people send up recommendations, and very seldom will I second-guess a good analyst."

But the process is not as hands-off as you might think. Mobius is on the road 80% of the time, he says, and has personally visited with the managers of all 500 companies that his funds and portfolios are invested in. That's saying quite a lot, considering that these companies are in 35 countries, and some aren't on the well traveled path. "I find that being on the road is more productive than being in an office," he said. "Someone has to make stops in all these countries and look at what's happening. This way I can talk face to face with the companies in which we invest and see what's happening."

John Neff

C ontrarian investing is an unnatural act, and John Neff spent a professional lifetime doing what most people's instincts tell them is wrong. He bought stocks when their prices were falling and the smart-money crowd was selling. And he let go of those stocks when they went on a roll.

When, at 64, Neff retired from managing Vanguard Windsor fund at the end of 1995, he'd been at that job 31½ years. And no veteran of such tenure on a fund (there aren't but a few) did any better. Across that span of time, Windsor returned about two percentage points per year more than the S&P 500. Doesn't sound like much, does it? But to outearn the larger market over a long span of time by even one percentage point is the unrealized dream of most money managers, and the effect of those two points since June of 1964 is the difference between a return of 4,973% (Windsor's) and 2,530% (the S&P 500's). The fund has been closed to new investors since the late 1980s.

The focus of this interview, conducted at the start of 1994 in Valley Forge, Pennsylvania, where Vanguard Group is headquartered, was, naturally enough, value investing, which Neff once described as buying "uncomfortable stocks . . . that make you twitch a bit."

KIPLINGER'S: Windsor has almost $11 billion in assets, yet it owns only 69 stocks. Aren't you taking a big risk by concentrating this way?

NEFF: We do hold large positions, and the risk we take is of poor short-term performance. But this is the sort of risk you should take, particularly if the stocks are woebegone, misunderstood and overlooked. You're not buying a lot of high hopes because investors aren't expecting much from these companies. We've gone so far as to tell shareholders that Windsor shouldn't be the only fund they own because we stick our necks out a bit.

In that respect, Windsor doesn't resemble an index fund—it's concentrated in financial and heavy-industrial stocks.

A couple of years ago, when this was a $7-billion fund, people assumed we were so big that we had to emulate the S&P 500. Well, of the 50 biggest stocks in the S&P, guess how many Windsor owned? None. Today, one or maybe two. We own relatively small companies like Seagate Technology and Conner Peripherals. In fact, we own 9.9% of Seagate.

Luckily, Seagate makes money.

That's the joy of it. The disk-drive industry is under considerable pressure. Usually the prices of drives go down 5% per quarter, and the makers offset that through productivity. The last several quarters, prices have declined 10%. All but one company is losing money; alone among them, Seagate is making decent profits. Now the price pressure is easing and Seagate could make $3.25 a share in '94. Our cost is $16 a share. The stock is at $24, and if it gets into the upper $20s we'll let some of it go.

You don't believe in letting your winning stocks run?

We have an enormous position in Seagate and we don't forget to sell into strength. A lot of people can't bear to sell when a stock's price is going up. They're convinced that they've made a mistake if they don't hold out for the last dollar.

My attitude is that we're not that smart. And you don't run big money that way. The same thing applies to a stock we want to buy that has been hosed. If you find 500,000 shares offered for $39.50 and think the company will do well a couple of quarters down the road, you can bid $39 and maybe get it. When you're after something nobody else wants, you can sometimes drive good bargains.

What's your thinking when choosing stocks?

Take aluminum as an example. The economy is growing moderately and capacity in aluminum isn't growing at all, because at today's price you only break even at best. No new capacity is in sight, while consumption is growing 3% to 5% worldwide. Our conviction is that the price of aluminum is going to have to go up. So we own big positions in Alcoa and Reynolds.

You try to keep your mind open to new stock-price opportunities and new evidence, and then act accordingly. For example, our bank position, which is large, had been exclusively in money-center banks—Citicorp, Bankers Trust, Chase and BankAmerica. We hadn't owned regional banks in eons. But now the regionals have been clocked. They're down 20% or 25% from their highs, and we're picking up four or five of them at good prices. We're getting them at seven or eight times next year's earnings, with yields of 4%, on average.

What sort of stress tests do you subject a stock to before buying it?

I look at the rate of earnings growth plus the dividend yield—that's how I define total return. I relate that to the stock's price-earnings ratio. The market usually ignores yield. Yet shareholders get that dividend.

Suppose a stock has an earnings growth of 10% and a yield of 4%, or 14% in all. What P/E ratio would you pay to buy it?

Maybe seven times earnings as of a year from now—half the rate of total return.

How do you calculate the growth rate of cyclical stocks, such as the aluminum companies, whose profits bounce up and down?

For these I figure "normalized earnings," which is what a company is capable of earning near the peak of a cycle. There are a lot of such stocks in the fund. With aluminums, we're saying that to justify new plant capacity, you'd need to have prices at 75 or 80 cents a pound, whereas they're only getting 51 cents now. At 80 cents a pound Alcoa would earn $12 a share and Reynolds $10. Those are normalized earnings.

In his book *The New Money Masters*, John Train said you will hold a stock "almost forever" to realize its value. Are you that patient an investor?

Yes, if the fundamentals are sustained. Now, if I'm wrong on those fundamentals . . .

Which raises the issue: When exactly will you sell a stock?

Everything we own was bought to be sold. If our predictions come to pass, and the market embraces a stock and it goes up, we start selling. That's simplistic but essentially the way I operate. If you get a significant price move, you begin selling early and look for something else. One reason the fund's cash level stays at around 20% is that we are consuming our ideas as we sell stocks.

Windsor fund badly underperformed the market in 1989 and 1990. Was your patience a factor?

Two things happened. First, financial stocks got killed—I thought unfairly—and I had 30% of our assets in those. Then tobaccos and drugs and household products and foods and telephones, all with ordinary growth rates, shot way up. We didn't own those stocks.

But you held on to the bank stocks. Back then, did you ever say to yourself, "Well, I made a big mistake. I'd better try another idea."

Oh, no. The fundamentals of the stocks were testy, but they were real. When stocks go down we're sometimes stupid enough to buy more. That's what we've always done. We do not listen to the marketplace. The only thing worse than being wrong is being whipsawed—you know, caving in at exactly the wrong moment and duplicating on the other side the losses you just suffered.

Did you get much grief from shareholders?

I got some letters, and in the 1990 shareholder report I responded to some that said I was an idiot to own thrifts and banks and insurance companies because everyone in the news media said they would go down. But you see, that's what we line up against—the conventional wisdom. Unfortunately, we were attracted to some of those stocks before they were beaten up. We bought Citicorp in the low $20s, and it went to $10. So did Chrysler.

Did you buy more of Citicorp and Chrysler all the way down?

We were willing to sit but you don't buy more when you've already made your bed. What we tried to do was find other things to buy.

Are you having trouble finding stocks to buy?

No. But I'm also not making much progress lowering our cash position, which is 20%, because I keep selling stocks, too. This market is unusual in that it has not been saw-toothed. Usually you would have had a price correction by now. I think a correction is overdue. But I guess it hasn't happened because you've been getting $8 billion to $10 billion a month of new money pouring into funds. This has helped to prop up the market.

Would you buy stocks during a correction?

Sure. That's what we did in 1987. I'm not afraid to buy into weakness because I've been doing it all these years. The day of the crash in 1987 we bought a couple hundred million dollars' worth of stocks.

Why haven't you bought health care stocks? Aren't they badly beaten up?

Being beaten up is the first qualification. But they still have to pass muster. We have big positions in Cigna, which runs the largest managed health care organization, and Aetna, which runs the second- or third-largest. We bought some hospitals, too. We haven't bought drug stocks. They are going to be impacted by Clinton's proposals. A couple of years ago, they got 9% and 10% price increases each year on existing drugs. Now they get maybe 3% or 3.5%. That takes a big hunk out of your growth rate.

You have a very well-defined investment style. Have you ever known anyone who flitted about in investing, like a bee among the flowers, with no discernible methods, who did make money?

You've got to have some sort of systematic approach or you won't know where you are. Although, speaking of flitting about, you can't forget the momentum school of investors. They key off of how well stocks are performing, whereas we are on the other side. That's a method, too, I guess, but it's awfully hard for me to understand. As best I can figure it, if a stock is going up that's good and if it's going down that's bad.

Will Rogers supposedly said, "I only buy stocks that go up; if they don't go up, I didn't buy them." Do you recall when you pretty much settled on the investing methods you used at Windsor?

Early on. I came out of a bank in Cleveland, where I had eight and a half rewarding years with good people and covered a wide area. I was an auto analyst and then did rubber and drugs and chemicals and finance and a couple of other things. But the bank's trust investment committee was dominated by a bond guy who reacted to stocks only after the fact instead of anticipating moves, so I left to join Wellington Management. They had this moribund fund, called Windsor, that had been killed in the 1962–'63 bear market.

At the time it followed an earnings-growth style of investing. I had this banking background that emphasized prudent-man principles, but also some willingness to take a bit of risk if the reward might be more than commensurate. So I changed the fund to emphasize low P/E ratios and kept it that way. I've always described my style as "four yards and a cloud of dust."

Once you settled into that groove, did you ever decide some of your methods weren't working quite right, and make some changes?

I always thought the market was wrong. My definition of an

irrational stock market is one in which Windsor doesn't do well. Seriously, you have to hang in there and sometimes wonder about yourself a little bit. We had a bad spell in 1971–'73, when the big growth stocks rolled away. Then in 1989 and 1990 the financial stocks got hit, and in 1990 it was all oil, energy and electronics. So you wonder in retrospect if you couldn't have tuned it up a little bit better.

There is a school of investing that rotates from sector to sector, but I always felt more comfortable with a continuous philosophy. Also, that philosophy is baked into the prospectus. The prospectus keeps most fund managers from tinkering too much with the way they do things.

Is there any chance we'll ever see a new mutual fund run by John Neff?

Oh, no. I won't last that long. I seem to be on top of my game. But your energy and dedication don't last forever. I'm going to go out with both guns blazing.

In rereading this interview before speaking to Neff in 1996, I realized that the first names to pop out of his mouth then were technology stocks. Was he an early celebrant at the big 1995 technology party? Not really, he said. "We were only about 5% invested in technology in 1994, which is a lot for a value fund. Conner Peripherals was taken over by Seagate, and we did well owning it. We bought Seagate at $24 a share and still own a lot of it at $60—we sold some, bought some back. Intel we made good money on, although we left some money on the table by selling well below its high, but I've done that before."

Windsor did well by its sizable investment in aluminum stocks, too. Alcoa doubled in price before being sold down substantially from the portfolio. "What hasn't worked as well is Reynolds Metals," Neff said. "In a homogeneous industry with close to a homogeneous record it's a little perplexing about Reynolds. So we simply bought more shares. I figure that stock still owes us something. But then, I'm speaking now about my former life."

In his last annual report to shareholders, Neff confessed to some disappointment that he had not ended his tenure at Windsor in the guns-blazing manner he wished. The fund about matched the S&P 500 in 1994 and trailed the index by seven percentage points in 1995, while still returning a respectable 30% that year. "It wasn't surprising in 1995," he said, "because when you get a breakout year like that, it's always hard for a fund like Windsor to keep up." Even so, his cloud-of-dust approach did better than two-thirds of the other growth-and-income funds. And just as sweet, the rest of the investment world finally thought as much of the big money-center banks as Neff, who wrote to shareholders in the dark days of 1990 that "a full 96% of our assets are *not* invested in Citicorp."

Michael Price

H e loves a deal. Show him a merger, buyout, spinoff, bankruptcy, restructuring or liquidation, and Michael Price or one of his analysts from Mutual Shares is sure to run the numbers and tote up asset values. His involvement may be limited to trying to squeeze the last $2-a-share profit out of a company that's being taken over. Or his fund may do the taking over itself. Price has bought entire companies whose assets he felt were grossly undervalued. In the pursuit of deals, the four Mutual Series funds have been unique.

Price's own career is unusual. In 1975, at age 23, he became the protégé of the late Max Heine, who was co-founder of Mutual Shares and a pioneer of mutual fund investing. Heine, too, loved deals, and the two developed a working relationship so close that Price eventually bought the investment-advisory business from the older man and followed the founder's investment methods so faithfully that the fund never skipped a beat.

When Price came aboard, Mutual Shares had $5 million in assets. At the start of 1996 he managed 2,600 times as much—$13 billion—in that fund and its sisters: Mutual Qualified, Mutual Beacon and Mutual Discovery. Mutual Shares, the oldest, delivered a 20% annualized total return over the 20 years to 1996—a staggering seven percentage points per year more than the typical growth and income fund, and five points more than Standard & Poor's 500-stock index.

If the story of Mutual Shares were that of one large triumph after another, it would be interesting enough. But Price's habit of taking huge positions in large companies he considers undervalued carries some risk. How he got involved in one buyout that turned sour was part of our initial conversation at the funds' offices in Short Hills, New Jersey, in 1993.

KIPLINGER'S: You're known as a value investor. Is that how you would characterize your funds?

PRICE: Two-thirds of each fund is value stocks. We take a conservative approach. We want to buy assets for 50 cents on the dollar. The other third is a combination of cash, bankruptcy investing—which is just a different approach to value investing—and deals.

And "deals" means . . .

Trading in stocks that are going through some form of restructuring. It could be a bankruptcy or merger or spinoff, or selling assets and using the proceeds to buy back stock. Other value-oriented funds stay away from deals. But I came from a deal-oriented background with Max Heine. We've always found opportunities trading in mergers and liquidations. We went through the inflation of the 1970s, the oil-price move and the liquidation of a lot of oil companies. I learned how to value companies in liquidation and how to trade in them. So I look for things in the market that I can exploit.

Where do you find your ideas?

In stocks that go down. From things that are bad news.

Is that how you found Sunbeam-Oster, which did so much for you in 1993?

Yes. Sunbeam came from Allegheny International, which went bankrupt. Before that, Allegheny had bought three companies that Mutual Shares had invested in—Chemetron, Sunbeam and Schenuit. Schenuit was a company out of Baltimore that made pallets, wheelbarrows, exercise equipment, skids and stuff like that—a $7 stock with a $15 book value, and run by the son-in-law of the founder.

A classic Mutual Shares stock!

Exactly. Max bought 76,000 shares for $7.50 in 1975. We got taken out by Allegheny at $35 in 1980. From then on we watched Allegheny, and by the time it went into Chapter 11 bankruptcy in 1988, we knew what was there. There was a great name inside

Allegheny—Sunbeam-Oster. Plus, there were a lot of businesses run by Allegheny that had been screwed up because they were lumped together the wrong way. When we laid it all out, we saw a lot of value.

By then, Allegheny had built up $300 million in cash. So on a 50/50 basis, we and [private investor] Mike Steinhardt offered $650 million for the company. We would use the cash inside the company, a bank loan and just $60 million each of our money. There were some other guys looking at Allegheny, so we bought the bank loans and the publicly owned debt, because once you own one-third of the debt you sort of have veto power over a bankruptcy reorganization plan.

Another bidder bought debt, too, and we had a standoff in court. The judge asked us both to raise our bids. We bumped ours up a bit and got the company. We paid $650 million, but by then it had $350 million in cash. The first thing we did was change the name from Allegheny to Sunbeam-Oster. Then in 1993 we brought Sunbeam public at $12.50 a share. Now the stock is at $17 and we're holding on to our stake—we love it. Today we carry stock at $600 million that we paid $30 million to own. The partnership made more than $1 billion profit on this deal.

Have you found many situations like this?

You find them, but since the funds have gotten larger, you need to find big ones to have a significant impact. If we can't invest $100 million, it's not worth it.

What about pure value stocks—are they rare birds, too?

That's why I started Mutual Discovery this year. A $7 stock with three million shares outstanding—you could never get enough of it in a $3-billion fund like Mutual Shares to make a difference. But Mutual Discovery has only $152 million in assets. It's a pocket for those small, cheap stocks—for 5,000 shares of a little bank in California that nobody ever heard of and is dirt cheap.

In Mutual Shares, Mutual Qualified and Mutual Beacon, what excites you now?

Sears and Kodak. We have big positions in both and are adding to them. Sears is restructuring, totally. They'll end up with retailing and Allstate Insurance. They're spinning off 20% of Allstate and selling all of Dean Witter Discover and Coldwell Banker. At today's $51 stock price, you're getting a $25-billion-a-year retailing business for nothing.

Why do you say that—because the spinoffs from Sears will realize $51 a share?

Exactly. Kodak is a little different. It has a medical-products business. It has Eastman Chemical. It has the film and x-ray business, an office-equipment business and about 30 other little things. When you value each business, you easily get to $70 a share. The stock is at $56. We bought two million shares and will end up with three or four million shares.

What's the cash position of your three older funds now?

In the mid teens. Cash is my security blanket. It goes up and down as we find things. If the market cracked this afternoon and Sears and Kodak and a few of our other favorite things came down, we'd go to 10% cash real quick.

You don't make calls on the stock market?
No.

Do you care what the economy is doing?

Sure I do. But I'm not trading stocks based on what I think will happen to the economy or based on my guess of the future of interest rates. I buy stocks only when they're available at the right price. If I do work on Baxter International and like it at $30, and the market, for whatever reason, brings Baxter down, I'd buy. I don't care what Clinton is going to do. I go by the numbers. Besides, the market overreacts one way or the other.

Could you give us an example?

Some mergers don't work. Medical Care America, which does outpatient surgery and kidney dialysis, merged with a company called Critical Care. The stock got as high as $70. Then, at $50 a share, they came in lower than expected on quarterly earnings. Earnings of the Critical Care side had caved in, and the stock went from $50 to $27 overnight, then bumped down to $17. This, by the way, is a debt-free company with a couple hundred million in cash.

We were looking it over and I went down to Dallas to see the chairman. His part of the company, the Medical Care part, is doing great, rolling out new outpatient centers in new towns. It's earning $1.60 a share. So the stock trades at ten times what his half of the company earns. You're getting the other half of the company for nothing, so it must be losing money, right? No. It's earning 60 cents a share. The Street was just looking for too much, and trashed the company. We bought stock at the $17 to $20 level, saw it go to $26 and sold some shares. Now it's at $24 and we're accumulating it again.

How did you establish the stock's value?

First, the balance sheet is clean. You have $200 million in cash. Then you value both businesses on earnings. You say, "I'll pay ten times earnings for the outpatient-surgery business. I'm paying nothing for the other half. It's clearly worth something." I arrive at a value of $35 to $40.

And there's your 50% discount. Any other good rules of thumb?

Once the price of Medical Care goes to $30, then what do you do? It's not 50 cents on the dollar anymore. That's when I start to skate on ice that's too thin for me. Sometimes we sell too early, but it's tough to know when to let go. On the buy side, all you need is a good stomach to keep buying when it's weak and nobody likes it.

Your funds went through a terrible period in 1989 and 1990. Was there a time when everyone around you thought you'd lost it?

June and July of 1989—that's when the music stopped, when the feds stopped banks from lending on deals. It was a costly, painful period. In 1990 I wrote down a huge Macy's investment, to one penny a share. That cost our funds more than $20 million. I sold Time Warner shares at a big loss—about $10 million. I would come to work in 1990 and see letters on my desk every day. "What kind of idiot are you, Mr. Price?" These were people who bought the fund in 1988 and early '89, when the price of our Macy's stock was way up and Time Warner was way up. Then our shareholders lost 5% in the last half of '89 and another 9% in 1990. Now they were saying, "Wait a minute! I thought this was a good fund."

What did you tell them?

What could I tell them? I'm not changing what I do. I did in 1989 through 1991 exactly what I did in 1985 and '80 and '87 and today. Max used to say, "With Mutual Shares, every ten years you'll have one great year, you'll have one horrible year and in the rest you'll do fine." To me, "fine" is the mid teens or better. In 1991, when the market was up 31% and our funds were up 21%, I was thrilled. I'm not out to beat the market. I'm looking to do 15% or more.

When things go wrong, do you question your methods?

All I know how to do in investing is this. So I ask whether I'm doing it right with respect to this stock or that.

Did you apply your methods correctly in helping take Macy's private?

Macy's was a mistake. But joining the leveraged buyout wasn't the mistake. Agreeing to let Macy's buy two other department-store chains after it was already leveraged was the mistake.

Let me tell you the story: In the fall of 1985 there was a rumor that Associated Dry Goods would make a bid for Macy's. To keep the company from being taken over and broken up, management got the help of Goldman Sachs and announced a $70-a-share LBO. Macy's had 60 stores—great name, spectacular ten-year track record, clean balance sheet, owned all its real estate, including three or four shopping centers.

Months pass. Nothing happens. I call Goldman: "You guys announced this LBO. Are you going to do it, or not?" They said, "Well, why don't you come talk about it?" So we did. I had watched people get really rich with LBOs. Mutual Shares had always been a value investor, selling shares to those LBO buyers who then got rich. I asked myself whether we should be on the other side this time.

The deal included a $900-million mortgage from Prudential, $600 million to $700 million in bank loans, and three bond issues—junk bonds with 14.5% to 16.5% coupons and some zero-coupon junk. It was these bonds that Goldman hadn't been able to sell.

We go to Macy's, get all the numbers, look at the books and start to hear their side of it—why, at $70 a share, it could work. We looked at other sources of funds if the business started to turn down. There were ten different backstops in case things went wrong.

So I'm standing on the main floor of Macy's at 34th Street— biggest store in the world—and the guy from Goldman looks at me and says, "Michael, do you think there's any chance of getting this done?" In other words, Goldman is really worried they couldn't finance this. I mean, they're the great investment bank. They'd been Macy's banker for 60 years. It had to work.

You talked to Larry Tisch, chairman of Loews Corp., about this, didn't you?

I told Larry what was happening. He said, "Michael, if you want to do this, I'll go 50/50 with you." So I called Goldman and said, "I'll buy this amount of junk bonds. But I want 25% of the company—the equity—for our funds and Loews." He calls back and says we got it. I said, "I also want a 16.5% coupon on all our junk bonds." He said fine.

That was February of 1986. The deal closed in July. We made $5 million or so arbitraging the stock during the buyout, and the junk bonds began trading at a big profit for us, netting us $12 million to $14 million. So the stock in the Macy's LBO cost us almost nothing.

Plus, you got a seat on Macy's board. When did the cracks appear?

In 1988. Macy's bought the Bullock's and I. Magnin department-store chains, and paid for them with expensive new debt. Then the department-store business turned south. Had it not bought those stores, Macy's could have made it through the bad economy without going bankrupt. It was a mistake. I should have voted against the deal. Clearly, it cost our funds money.

How directly involved are you in buy and sell decisions for the funds?

One hundred percent. I sit out on the trading desk. We all sit together and are constantly talking about the price at which we want to be buying a stock, or the price at which we want to sell.

How much time do you work each week?

A lot. But more to the point is how you spend the time. It's asking the right questions and thinking the right way. You may spend ten minutes reading the president's letter in an annual report. It's all garbage. I like to read an annual report backward, starting with the last footnote to the financial statement and going up. Note 17 will say, "In 1992 we got a letter from the EPA that we're a responsible party for a Superfund site in Missouri." Note 16: "The IRS has audited our 1986, '87 and '88 returns and wants $300 million." Note 15, and so on. None of that will be in the president's letter. I'm serious! I owe that bit of advice to Max Heine.

What was the best advice Max ever gave?

There actually wasn't a lot of advice. He would set examples. And the best example he ever set for me—that you never see on Wall Street—was his lack of arrogance. Max was a terrific guy, terrific investor, sweetheart of a person. He carried zero arrogance. A shareholder who calls today and asks for me will either get me on the phone or, if I'm tied up, one of the two or three top people. I work for them.

"Do you feel sort of left out in a year like 1995?" I asked Price when we spoke at the end of that year. His response? "No. We had a pickup in merger activity. A lot of our 'situations' worked out extremely well. Our funds were up 27, 28%. We're ending the year 25% in cash and with no technology stocks. Our shareholders got a good deal in 1995. You see, everyone makes money in bull markets. The key is what they do in tough years, like 1994, when we were up 7% and 8% and so many other funds had losses."

In the 21 months since the original interview, Price had been busy. Kodak was gone from the portfolios. "It traded up and we took our profits. We were there for its chairman to spin off Eastman Chemical, sell the drug business and close down other pieces. The stock went from $40 a share to $60, plus the value of the spinoffs, which puts it to $75." Sears remained a big holding, and the Mutual Series funds at least doubled their money on it and the subsidiaries it spun off as separate companies. The funds still owned 17 million shares of Sunbeam-Oster; counting money realized from earlier sales, the original $60 million investment had spawned realized and unrealized gains of $500 million. But when Macy's was bought out of bankruptcy in 1995 by Federated Department Stores, the funds' 25% ownership was wiped out, as Price had predicted it would be.

The two biggest deals of Price's career occurred in 1995 and 1996. First, his funds bought 11.5 million shares of Chase Manhattan at $35, then began pressuring the bank to "unlock" some of the value in the stock. Within months, Chase agreed to merge with Chemical, and the price surged to $40, then $50 and beyond $60 a share. In less than a year, the Mutual Series funds came close to doubling an investment of more than one-third of a billion dollars. And they were about to buy a one-fourth interest in the financially troubled Canary Wharf office complex in London, for $160 million.

When Price went to work for Max Heine, just the two of them ran the whole fund. By 1996, he had 15 analysts at his beck and call. At age 44, did Mike Price feel as if he'd done it all? "I hear ya," he replied. "Being a portfolio manager with the flexibility to go where the action is—that's what I like. I never get bored. The job is fun. This is like a 24-hour-a-day IQ game."

Soon thereafter it became obvious that Price wanted to get involved in deals with his own money as well as that of the funds. Early in 1996 he hired an investment bank to seek a buyer for Heine Securities, the advisory firm he owned that manages the Mutual Series funds. That summer he struck a deal to sell Heine to the Franklin/Templeton fund group for a price that could ultimately reach $800 million. And whether Price will remain involved in these funds for the long term—beyond the next two years—remains to be seen. If not, the question will be whether he taught his long-time lieutenants this brand of investing as thoroughly as Max Heine taught him.

Robert Sanborn

Robert Sanborn lives and invests by the value code. "I was
a Filene's Basement kind of kid growing up in Boston,"
says the manager of Oakmark fund. "I like bargains in
anything." Sanborn, born in 1958, had no experience at a
mutual fund before he began with Oakmark. But he has already
become something of a legend among value investors because of
the fund's stunning results. In its first full calendar year, 1992, it
outearned the S&P 500-stock index by 40 percentage points, and in
its second year by 20 points.

Oakmark was one of the early examples in the 1990s of what's
known as the "new fund effect." Perhaps because they can concentrate their bets, there is a tendency for some new funds to
achieve stunning results right out of the box. Later, as the fund
grows, the total return tends to gravitate toward the mean. This
certainly was the case with Oakmark. Actually, there was a
perception that Oakmark's meteoric return in 1992 occurred
because of some obscure investment he made early on. And as it
turned out, it did, as we learned in this interview, which occurred in
Chicago in the spring of 1995.

**KIPLINGER'S: You seemed to come out of the woodwork in
1991. Had you harbored ambitions of running a fund?**

SANBORN: It was my goal almost from the time I entered
business school at the University of Chicago. I worked for a couple of
years for the State Teachers Retirement System of Ohio and got to
see a variety of money-managing styles. I learned what worked and
what didn't work.

What didn't work?

Well, one guy invested by reading the charts, and I could never
tell from looking at a chart whether it was a good stock or not.

Another was an earnings-momentum guy trying to buy quarterly earnings at a higher growth rate than . . . whatever. There was no intellectual coherence to his method.

Then did you stumble upon someone investing just the way you wanted to invest?

Not really. But the sum of these experiences was to confirm my value philosophy. The methods I use sort of evolved over time. When I came here to Harris Associates in 1988, my goal was to work as a backup for one of the managers handling the private accounts. But I discovered it wasn't what I wanted to do, after all. So some of us began advocating that Harris start a new mutual fund with a value philosophy, and when it did, I was picked to manage it.

Although you're a value investor, you pay no attention to price-earnings ratios or price-to-book-value ratios, do you?

None at all. The core philosophy is to buy stocks of companies at a large discount to their underlying value. And the underlying value is what a rational businessperson would pay to own the whole enterprise. There's nothing proprietary here. A number of people do the same thing. (See the interview with Donald Yacktman, beginning on page 165.)

How do you calculate underlying value?

First of all, we look very carefully at all transactions affecting companies similar to those we are analyzing. By transactions I mean when companies are bought out and taken private, or when businesses are spun off by their parent companies, or when one company buys another.

Sounds like how a tax assessor fixes home values by looking at sales of similar homes.

Exactly. We look very carefully at the values associated with those acquisitions—the price per unit of sales, the price to discretionary cash flow, and so forth. Discretionary cash flow means pretax earnings plus depreciation minus capital spending needed to maintain the existing business. And we try to understand the assumptions underlying those values.

At how much of a discount to their private market values do you like to buy stocks?

Ideally, at 60% or less, and we sell the stocks when they reach 90% of underlying value. The classic example—and the one that made our record in 1992—is Liberty Media, a cable-TV company spun off by Tele-Communications Inc. in a transaction that was the most complicated I've ever seen. The price at which it would be spun off would be determined, in part, by how many TCI shareholders elected to transfer their stock to Liberty. The conventional wisdom was that the company would be too small and that TCI was putting some of its dross into Liberty.

The situation was ripe for Liberty to come out at a very low price. The prospectus would describe a small programming operation within Liberty and say that similar public companies were valued at ten times cash flow, but it was small so its value would be discounted. Every part of the company was discounted, and when the pieces were put together, the sum total was discounted, too! They were doing haircuts on top of haircuts, and they ended up giving the thing away for less than 50% of its value.

Liberty was one of our biggest holdings. By the time TCI bought it back in 1994, I think we'd made 24 times our investment.

Why invest solely on the basis of private market value? Most publicly owned companies are not taken private.

A stock is a piece of ownership of a business, and the value of that business is what someone will pay to own it. Sooner or later, for our markets to work—and we have the most efficient market system in the world—price and value must converge. If they do not, then there are people who will force the issue. If a stock is trading at $50 and is really worth $100, some entrepreneurial people will buy the whole thing for $75 a share and make a lot of money. So that's what we focus on.

Your method implies a lot of number-crunching and not a lot of judgment. Where does science end and art begin?

Our judgment is in terms of the quality of the business—where the values will be long term—and in the quality of management. We like to meet them face to face, and hear a coherent strategy that tells me they understand the dynamics of their business. Is it worthy of reinvestment of profits? Good managers will know. Kmart reinvested its profits in the business and at best got subnormal returns, and perhaps negative returns.

The second thing we want is management whose interests are aligned with ours. I want them to own a lot of the stock, preferably with their own money rather than through stock options. They should get some money for showing up, but the real serious money should be for increasing the value.

Getting back to the start of the fund, was it the beneficiary of the "new-fund effect," and if so, just what is that effect?

I don't know. One of the misconceptions about Oakmark fund is that it was a small-company fund. It really wasn't. On day one we had $100,000, and the three stocks I bought were large-capitalization issues that I still own: TCI, Philip Morris and American Home Products.

I guess people think that with a new mutual fund you can start out fresh and invest only in good ideas. But you should be able to do that with your portfolio every Monday morning.

On that note, is there one stock that you wish you could put all of Oakmark's money in?

First USA is the stock that I think is tremendous. If I owned only two stocks, they would be First USA and Philip Morris.

First USA is already 6% of Oakmark's assets. Doesn't it process bankcard transactions?

Yes. And it issues bankcards, too. It's a great business, it's misunderstood by Wall Street, the valuation is still very inexpensive and

management owns a ton of the stock. Right now it trades at $37, and
we think the value is probably $60.

**What's so attractive about Philip Morris? Look at all the
restrictions on smoking and the lawsuits coming in. How can
you be so upbeat about the stock?**
The restrictions I don't worry about. That's over. I mean, what
else can they do to smokers? And you know, smokers are one-fourth
of American adults.

Are there growth opportunities for tobacco overseas?
Oh, it's huge overseas. I know people think this is weird, but
there has never been any clinical proof of cigarettes causing
problems; it's all statistical. The Japanese, I think, have shown that if
you combine smoking with a low-fat diet, it's not a problem. It's
smoking with a high-fat diet that's the problem.

Can't you just see the headline? "Sanborn . . ."
". . . is a nut."

"Sanborn Says Smoking Is Fine—Just Eat Lots of Rice."
It hasn't been proven. It's true.

You don't own technology stocks. Is that deliberate?
Like Freddy Krueger, who keeps coming back to Elm Street, this
is an issue that won't go away for Harris Associates. Every three
months an analyst will come up with a tech stock with great cash
flow, a leading position in its field, cash on the balance sheet net of
debt and a price that's down from $50 to $30. A couple of people here
will say, "Look, Bob, this is value!" And I'll say, "Yes, but this business
could be gone in five years." I've always had a very hard time with
technology. I don't understand it. It takes too much skill to learn a
technology company.

But these companies are reshaping the world we live in.

Aren't you handicapping the fund?

Not at all. In 1982, when I got in this business, I remember the guys from Prudential-Bache were coming around. They had companies like Hogan Systems and a bunch of other names I can't remember that they talked about in a half-day seminar. Every single stock among the 100 or so technology companies that were discussed was rated a "buy" for both the short and long term. I remember thinking, "Boy, is it this easy to make money in these things?" The thesis then was that the PC boom would affect every desktop in American business.

The thesis was correct. But if you had bought those stocks any time in the early 1980s you would have underperformed the overall stock market hugely. The problem isn't that these computer companies aren't reshaping the world, because they are, but that it's tough to make money in those businesses in the long run because of obsolescence, the need for huge R&D outlays, write-offs and all the rest of it. I'd rather invest in the companies that exploit the technology, not the ones that own it.

Is Oakmark, with $1.2 billion in assets, getting too big?

The capacity to overperform, and to underperform, is greater with a small asset size—no doubt about that. I'm trying to grapple with that. It's a tough situation. We've never advertised Oakmark fund—the money keeps coming in and we manage to stabilize things. But the growth of assets has been pretty sedate the past year.

So you think you could invest a lot of additional money?

I think we could add value.

What does "add value" mean?

That over the long run we can outperform the S&P 500 index significantly, with less volatility.

In other words, you're opposed to closing Oakmark to new investors?

It's not my personal decision to make, but the trustees', of which I am one. At the current time we can add value, as long as growth is moderate and reasonably consistent.

You beat the S&P 500 by only two percentage points in 1994. . .

Two or three percentage points every year is huge. This is a very competitive business. If we outperformed the S&P every year like we did in 1991–'93, we'd own the world.

One hallmark of your fund seems to be a willingness to make big bets. Is that true?

I want the 20 biggest holdings to make up 65% of the fund. For the other 35%, it could be 100 companies, or whatever. I look at the other 35% as a basket of cheap, small companies. We follow each of them reasonably closely. We visit the management teams and talk to them. But we don't give them the same level of scrutiny we give our top ten or 15 holdings.

Concentration is the way to go. I would like to be concentrated in even fewer stocks.

Doesn't that sometimes scare you?

Not really. What's riskier: owning 20 stocks that you know really well and that are priced right, or owning 500 stocks that you don't know that well, some of which are priced at insane levels?

But isn't it preordained that a fund that is as concentrated as yours is going to walk off the side of the cliff someday?

We're going to have short periods when concentration hurts us. I want shareholders to have a five-year time frame and be able to tolerate a 20% loss.

How many stocks do you yourself own?

None. Harris Associates has always been very careful ethically. If you are going to tell shareholders that you buy shares of companies with owner-oriented management, they have the right to ask the same thing of you. So excluding my house, my investments are essentially 70% Oakmark and 30% Oakmark International.

Just those two funds?

Plus very small amounts in a few others, in order to get their annual reports. I think people tend to overdiversify their funds. Ten is too many. If you own a value fund, a growth fund, an international fund, an emerging-markets fund and, as you get older, a fixed-income fund, that's all you need.

The ink from this interview was still wet when the letters started coming in. How dare we, some readers asked, make respectable this crackpot who maintains that cigarettes don't cause cancer? *Kiplinger's* published one of the most indignant of those letters. I asked Sanborn if he wanted to respond. Not at all, he answered. "I'd just tell him to get a life." Then he laughed.

This is pure Robert Sanborn—opinionated, and proud of it. Ask him a question and the words pour out so fast that he has to keep backing up to start his sentences over again, because the mind outruns the mouth. Oakmark's shareholder reports are never boring, either. In one he declared his political credo to be libertarian. In another he wrote an essay on investment manias.

For a value fund, Oakmark did well in 1995, returning 34% to the S&P 500's 38%. "We're not a bull-market fund," he said. "We had a good year, given our style. If Oakmark had one-tenth the assets, it would have been the same, or maybe worse, because we would have owned more small-company stocks and they didn't do well in 1995."

The stocks Oakmark owned in 1995 were still the stocks it owned in 1996—just a lot pricier. For instance, First USA, trading at $37 then, was at $52 early in 1996. Was its private market value (PMV) still $60, and if so, was it almost time to say goodbye to First USA? Sanborn replied that the PMV of First USA had risen, to $78. "The stock market's big move was explained entirely by lower interest rates, he declared. "Stocks at the end of 1995 were no more expensive than they were in 1994, because the cost of money had come down and the value of a company's earnings had risen. The private market value of Philip Morris is now $150 [with a share price of $92.63 in early 1996], and Tele-Communications is $29 [share price, $21.13]. I'm not near to selling any of them."

Kent Simons
& Larry Marx

Were they going to the dogs? As the market went up in 1996, Neuberger & Berman Guardian fund just sat there, not going down but not going up much, either. This pretty much describes the fund's behavior all year. Did it worry Kent Simons and Larry Marx? Yes, but it shouldn't have. The essence of value investing, which is what they do very well, is betting against the crowd by buying stocks that appear to be undeservedly cheap. And the price you pay is sometimes being a wallflower at the prom. Not to worry: Over the past five, ten and 15 years, Guardian has done better than the stock market as a whole.

Simons, born in 1935, succeeded Guardian founder Roy Neuberger at this fund in 1981. He was joined by co-manager Larry Marx III, 11 years his junior, in 1988. (Neuberger analyst Kevin Riesen made the duo a trio in 1996.) Their working arrangement is worthy of note: Simons (and now Riesen as well) operates out of New York City, while Marx holds forth at that other citadel of American capitalism, Aspen, Colorado. That's where we met in April of 1996.

KIPLINGER'S: Guardian is known for seeking out woebegone, undervalued stocks. So what are technology stocks like Compaq and Texas Instruments doing among your biggest holdings? Are you buying growth stocks without telling each other?

MARX: You call these technology companies growth stocks. There's this conception that value-driven guys aren't allowed to own them . . .

Isn't it against the law?

MARX: If you look at how these companies are valued—whether it's the price-earnings ratio or price-to-cash-flow ratio—they met our standards as value companies when we bought them. And we like to own good, growing companies like these.

SIMONS: The primary thing we look at is the P/E ratio—what we call the valuation. So Larry's right. People may call these growth stocks, but when we bought them they traded at ten times earnings when the stock market as a whole traded for 16 or 17 times earnings.

So your definition of an undervalued stock is one with a low P/E ratio?

MARX: That, or a low ratio of price to cash flow. There's no absolute number. We want the P/E to be low in relation to the overall stock market, or low in comparison with the company's rate of earnings growth.

How does an undervalued company make it onto your radarscope?

SIMONS: Most people know what's cheap. It's no secret that technology is out of favor. It was no secret in the fourth quarter of 1995 that everyone was worried about credit card companies. It's just a matter of taking the time to differentiate between the ones that deserve to be cheap and the ones that don't.

Companies become cheap three ways. They can fall out of favor by being out of sync with the economic cycle—steady-growth companies at a time when the economy is expanding, or cyclical companies when the economy is contracting. They can fall out because of an earnings disappointment, and these days you'd have to live in a cave to miss those. I guess the hard ones to find are those that reach attractive values because of neglect.

For example?

SIMONS: A whole new little industry was created after Hurricane Andrew—the Bermuda companies that provide catastrophe reinsurance. There are eight such companies, and five are publicly owned. Only three analysts follow these stocks, and two of them work for little boutique securities firms in Hartford. The stocks sell at six times earnings. That's a case of neglect.

So after you've identified a bunch of companies that fit your P/E parameter, then what?

MARX: Then we ask, should we buy these? Or was the market right to value them so cheaply? It's a case of rolling up your sleeves, talking to managements, talking to the better people on Wall Street and getting comfortable with the names. If you know where to look, you can find good people who know the companies and who can help you understand them. This can be difficult with industries such as the one Kent just mentioned that are new to us. But when Wall Street perceived that Mrs. Clinton was going to put the pharmaceutical companies out of business, there wasn't nearly as much legwork that needed doing before we became buyers.

When we buy a stock, we have a set of assumptions about that company—in other words, reasons we are buying it. We aren't arrogant enough to think we can predict earnings that well, or know where the P/E multiple will go. But we do make assumptions such as that the company is gaining market share or achieving a certain return on investment or what have you.

Do you or Neuberger & Berman's analysts spend a lot of time working up estimates of future earnings?

MARX: We rely on Wall Street analysts for earnings models. We don't bother managements about each week's sales and gross margins.

So it's fair to say you spend your time thinking and talking about a company rather than filling in spreadsheets?

MARX: That's 100% accurate.

Could you explain how you applied these methods to a stock you recently bought?

SIMONS: Barnes & Noble, the bookseller. Its stock went

public in 1993 at $23 per share, and went right to $42. I thought that was too much, especially for a company that earns money only in the fourth quarter because of the seasonal nature of its business. Then the stock went down to $24, and I'll look at anything that goes from $42 to $24. They're supposed to earn $1.40 in 1996, so the price is in line with the market's P/E. I arranged for several of us from Neuberger to meet with the company's chief financial officer late one Friday afternoon. He said he would give us an hour. We stayed for two.

Well, it turns out the bookstore business is pretty interesting. Sales for the industry are rising 6% to 8% a year, and everything they don't sell can be sent right back to the publisher. And the growth rate is accelerating. Why? Because everybody used to own little bookstores, and now they're opening superstores. Plus, there are really only two companies, Barnes & Noble and Borders.

What Barnes & Noble does makes a lot of sense. They're closing down stores in shopping malls—where they go under the name B. Dalton—and opening superstores under the Barnes & Noble name. These cost, on average, $1.8 million, and by the fourth year their return on investment is quite high. Because they're expanding so rapidly, the depreciation charge is really enormous.

But depreciation cuts earnings, not the cash flow.

SIMONS: Exactly. I said to the CFO: "Here's a company that one man has run for 25 years, 23 of them privately. It strikes me that owners of private businesses don't run them to ring up profits, but for the cash returns," and the CFO basically agreed. The cash flow is $3.20 per share, versus reported earnings of $1.40, and cash flow is increasing at a 30% annual rate. We value the company on cash flow, because this is how it is run. If he could, the CEO, Lenny Riggio, would report no profit at all.

You also run a second fund, Neuberger & Berman Focus, which is sort of a distilled version of Guardian. Are you surprised that Focus outperformed Guardian each year since

you overhauled its investment parameters in 1991?

MARX: No. In 1995, the stocks in Guardian returned more than those in Focus. But Guardian was lugging a lot of cash around and overall didn't do quite as well. Over time, you would expect that good midsize or small companies, which Focus owns [in addition to larger names], will do better than good large companies, which Guardian owns.

Would you advise your friends to invest in Focus rather than Guardian?

MARX: Yes, if they are prepared to accept a degree more volatility.

Why has Guardian underperformed the overall market in late 1996 and early 1996? Did you make some big mistakes?

Marx: We're doing the same things. For the time being, they're just not producing superior results. Some of the things we invest in came under pressure—namely, the tech stocks.

If the fund isn't doing well, when do you begin asking yourself if you did something wrong?

SIMONS: About the second or third day. It's interesting: In the third quarter of 1995, Guardian was in the top 1% of funds in total return. In the fourth quarter it was in the bottom 6%. And the stocks were pretty much the same. The market has gone up, and we've been flat. But it's not as if someone hit us on the head with a stick and we went daffy.

But at what point do you go from being disciplined to just plain old stubborn?

SIMONS: When it's working you're called courageous and patient, and when it isn't you're called stubborn and stupid. It's no fun to underperform. Nobody likes owning stocks that go down. I hear interviews with managers who just dumped all their tech stocks or threw out all their credit card stocks. What comes across to me is that they didn't want to own the stuff that was going down, and later they made up the reasons these stocks were no good anymore. But our record over the long term proves we're doing what we should be doing.

You could say I was a genius buying drug stocks in 1993. But it wasn't easy at the time. And there come moments when I will turn to Larry and say, "Am I missing something here?" We turn to each other at crisis points. Larry has asked me, "What do you think about these technology stocks?" because those are his babies. And I say, "I'd own them all." That's what we do—when Texas Instruments goes down, everybody hates it, and we are buyers. My guess is that a year from now people will say, "Well, sure, buying TI at $50—that was a no-brainer." Well, let me tell you, pal, it's not easy.

Inevitably, there must be times when you disagree with the other person's decision to buy or sell . . .

SIMONS: No. Never. Honestly, I've never felt that.

MARX: It's really important. This is a stressful business if you do it the way we do. You can't last if you don't have the support of your co-managers. I'd absolutely cave. Too many people in this business like beating up on each other. That's what results in bad investment decisions.

SIMONS: Not to mention unsolved murders.

I think I know why Simon and Marx stay half a continent apart: To be in a room with Larry Marx as he works is almost unbearable. The man is like a caged tiger, a bundle of pent-up energy and raw nerve endings. As the interview progressed, Larry flexed his fingers, his hands, his legs. He strode back and forth across his in-home office. He joked that he runs up the mountain outside his office at noontimes to work off the tension he lives with. Maybe it isn't a joke.

I thought of Larry in particular as the year 1996 progressed. Each year turns out to have a unique investing climate, and whatever else you can say of 1996, it was not a Marx-and-Simons kind of year. By November, Guardian's year-to-date total return had crept up to 13%—not bad in itself, but still far short of the S&P 500 index, which was up almost 20%.

"When it's working you're called courageous and patient," Simons had said of their investing methodology, "and when it isn't you're stubborn and stupid." How very true. This was their year to appear stubborn and stupid. What could they do about it? Nothing, except to pay even more attention to the fundamentals of their stock-picking style, and await deliverance.

Roland Whitridge

How he got the job: The directors of David L. Babson & Co. decided in 1983 to start a fund specializing in undervalued stocks. But who would run it? The firm's expertise, it seemed, was investing in fast-growing companies. As Roland "Nick" Whitridge tells it, one director said, " 'Let's let Nick do it—he's always complaining that we pay too much for stocks.' "

And they did. So Whitridge, who was not then a value investor, had to figure out how to become one. He came up with a methodology for running Babson Value that was so effective he has never needed to alter it. Among growth-and-income funds, his ranked in the first decile for total return during the past three, five and ten years.

What's more, says Whitridge, born in 1938, you can invest the same way he does. All you need is a good computer data base and an irrational mind-set. But we're getting ahead of ourselves. This interview took place in Whitridge's small, paper-strewn office overlooking the Charles River in Cambridge, Massachusetts, in the autumn of 1996.

KIPLINGER'S: The thing you quickly notice about Babson Value is that it always owns 40 stocks, give or take a few, and that it owns almost equal dollar amounts in each of them. What's the reason?

WHITRIDGE: When I was in graduate school, they told us you could get adequate diversification with 20 to 25 stocks. That seemed a bit narrow to me, for a fund. Yet with 60 to 100 stocks, no single stock can make that much of a difference. So holding 40 issues is a compromise. And I continually rebalance the portfolio to give each stock an equal dollar weighting.

So instead of cutting your losers and letting your winners run, you do the opposite?

When you let your winners run, you end up with a portfolio dominated by a very few stocks. One of these days those companies are going to report earnings a nickel below what analysts expect and you are going to lose a lot of money in the downdraft. What I do defies Wall Street logic, but it seems to work.

You see, I cannot tell which of the 40 stocks the fund owns will do best in the next 12 months. Far better to let all the stocks have an equal chance of producing good results for the overall portfolio.

How do you find candidates for replacing a stock?

By screening a data base of 1,250 stocks—essentially, issues in Standard & Poor's 500-stock index plus 750 others. My purpose is to reduce the list of possible investments to a reasonable number, 65, so that our analysts can give them a closer look.

What attributes are you looking for?

I score them equally on ten statistics. The first five are signposts of undervalued stocks: the company's current price-earnings ratio; its current P/E relative to its average P/E the past 15 years, with an extra weighting given to the average of the past five years; its current ratio of price to book value; its average price-to-book ratio the past 15 years; and its dividend yield. The other five measures have to do with earnings growth—a terrible term!

Your secret is safe with us. But aren't you looking for undervalued stocks?

Everybody knows that value investors tend to get into stocks way too early. So I'm trying to identify companies that are statistically cheap but that have something happening on the earnings side to give us hope they are coming out of their trough. I still buy companies too early, but this may help.

The first benchmark is the percentage change in earnings from the prior 12 months compared with the estimated earnings of the next 12 months. The second is earnings momentum and involves no guesswork: It is the percentage change in earnings from the trailing

12 months in the previous quarter to the trailing 12 months in the latest quarter. Then there's earnings surprise: the difference between the consensus earnings estimate of analysts before the most recent quarter and the actual reported number.

Are you sure this isn't Babson Growth fund?

Bear with me. The fourth measure is a guess at the sustainable growth rate of a company without outside financing. And I do it by figuring the stock's reinvestment rate—earnings minus dividends paid out—as a percentage of book value. So if a company is expected to earn $1 a share in the next 12 months and pay a dividend of 10 cents a share, its retained earnings are 90 cents a share, which you divide by book value per share.

Finally, there's the dividend-payout ratio—the percentage of earnings paid out as dividends. The lower the better. I don't want to end up owning only utility companies.

Now you take those 1,250 companies, rank 'em equally on all ten selectors, add up all the points and throw out the bottom 80% of those stocks. That leaves me with 250 stocks, which is still too many.

So I rescreen all the survivors, but this time I use only the five value measures. You see, I've already identified statistically cheap stocks in which something positive may be happening in earnings. Now I want to know which of those are the cheapest. And I throw out the three-fourths that score the lowest, leaving me with 65 stocks.

Why 65? Why not 35? After all, you're not trying to replace your whole portfolio—just select one stock to replace one you've sold.

The reason is very scientific. The computer program lists 13 stocks per page when I print it out, and I can fill five pages with no wasted space. And I give these names to our 15 analysts to work on.

What do you seek from your analysts?

I want them to confirm that the numbers that got the company through the screening process are valid, so that we don't deal with statistical garbage. And I want them to use their analytical wiles to tell me which companies we can have the most confidence in. All this to replace six to eight stocks a year.

What is the trickiest part of your procedure?

The final choice. Typically, I'll have half a dozen companies that look best. I usually go with the company that will best improve the diversification of the portfolio. Right now, 30% of assets are in financial stocks. That's two and a half times the weighting of financial stocks in the S&P 500, and I don't want to add another one unless I sell a financial stock. I'll look for a stock in an industry where I'm underweighted.

Is Kmart a good example of Babson Value's investment process?

We bought Kmart and then it kept dropping with all the negative news. So the question was whether to keep it. I called suppliers that sell their products through Kmart and asked, "Have you changed your credit policy toward Kmart because of all the stuff we read in the newspapers?" And they all said no—that Kmart paid its bills on time. Well, that, combined with the fact that same-store sales were going up and total sales were going up, gave me confidence. Kmart didn't smell like a company about to go out of business. And it became a big winner in the past year.

What stock gives you the most heartburn today?

Apple Computer. We bought it early in 1995, in the low $30s, and in three weeks it went to $50. I thought I was a genius. Now it's $21. We bought Apple when the whole world was focused on the introduction of Windows 95, which was going to put Apple out of business. Then the Wall Street Journal had a story the other day saying that a lot of corporations are giving up on Apple's Macintosh, which makes me feel even more alone. But I think Apple still has a very loyal customer base. The new CEO is trying to right-size the company. Its problems were really related to production and marketing.

So Apple is a stock that once looked cheap but now looks expensive because the earnings disappeared. You have to look across the valley. If at some point I decide that the valley is just too wide, it may be one that we sell.

Could a conscientious individual investor replicate your methods?

I think so. You could use Morningstar's *U.S. Equities OnFloppy* data base to start. What I do is simple, but it's not easy, and the reason is that old human-nature thing. I have to buy stocks that everyone knows have problems. That's what creates the opportunity for me. But I'm human, too! If I were totally comfortable with every stock I own, I probably wouldn't have very many good opportunities in the portfolio.

How many times have you said to yourself that you could not possibly be as good a stock picker as the successful mutual fund managers you read about? It's true that some managers rely heavily on decades of knowledge about certain companies, that others have access to companies' senior management that ordinary investors lack, and that a few use expensive data bases.

But in Nick Whitridge you get the whole ball of wax, start to finish. No secrets withheld. No access to data you can't get yourself. No mumbo jumbo. If you stand back from the details of what he does, you can see the aspects of his investment style that have made it succeed:

- **He devised stock-picking methods that were logical** and, more important, that he felt comfortable with.

- **He follows that process come what may.** To put it another way, he has discipline.

- **He's aware that he must act contrary to his own nature** by embracing stocks that most people would avoid.

  There you have it. So what are you waiting for?

The Growth Investors

Lawrence Auriana & Hans Utsch

Robert Bacarella

Elizabeth Bramwell

James Craig

Shelby Davis

Foster Friess

Rod Linafelter

Gary Pilgrim

James Stowers III

Garrett Van Wagoner

Ralph Wanger

Donald Yacktman

G rowth investing is easy to define, which probably explains why it's so popular. It is grounded on the assumption that profits are what moves stock prices. This is undeniable. If a company whose stock is at $10 a share increases its earnings in a year's time from $1 a share to $4, its stock price will undoubtedly reflect that change. Maybe it will go to $40; if conditions are right, it could touch $100. Therefore, the growth investor buys stocks of companies whose earnings are increasing.

But what looks easy really isn't. News about rising earnings gets out quickly. Before you know it, that $10 stock is already at $40, in anticipation of those $4 in profits that are still on their way. Let the earnings growth falter—let Wall Street even *think* the earnings growth will falter—and the stock could be on its way back to $10. On the other hand, let that $4 per share profit become $5 a share instead and you could have a $100 stock very quickly.

Larry Auriana and partner Hans Utsch, Foster Friess, Gary Pilgrim, Jim Stowers and Garrett Van Wagoner stand at the no-holds-barred end of the growth-stock spectrum. Friess (Brandywine fund), Pilgrim (PBHG funds) and Stowers (Twentieth Century funds) are momentum investors. They invest in stocks because their prices and earnings are rising; they sell when earnings and price lose that momentum. Rewards are high, but so are risks. As you will discover, all three put their organizations under tremendous stress to identify winners quickly. Auriana and Utsch (Kaufmann fund) get their edge by standing beside the starting gate. They specialize in IPOs—the initial public offerings of companies just entering public ownership. The best ones Auriana and Utsch buy and buy, and hold and hold. Van Wagoner's judgement is buttressed by his extensive knowledge of the high-tech industries he exists in; when they're hot, he's hot.

At the conservative end of growth-stock investing are James Craig, Shelby Davis and Donald Yacktman. Craig (Janus fund) wants stocks whose earnings growth is predictable a couple of years hence, and that are underappreciated by the rest of the investing world. Davis (Davis New York Venture) likes growing companies whose profitability comes under a cloud of suspicion; when the cloud lifts, he'll have bought 3% of the shares. Yacktman prefers companies that require little capital—the Philip Morrises, Reeboks and Cloroxes of this world. As a buyer, he's a cheapskate. But by their nature these companies are fast growers. Yacktman fund has been a growth fund in the hands of a value investor.

Between the two poles stand Robert Bacarella (Monetta), Elizabeth Bramwell (Bramwell Growth), Rod Linafelter (Berger One Hundred) and Ralph Wanger (Acorn funds). This quartet uses spreadsheets and shoe leather to identify companies with growing profits. It's interesting to note that of these four, all but Wanger started running their first fund in the last half of the 1980s (or in Linafelter's case, 1990). Although they all say it isn't so, one suspects that their methods are still evolving.

Larry Auriana
& Hans Utsch

Kaufmann fund occupies a niche all its own. Almost every stock in its portfolio got there during an initial public offering. Using IPOs as their source of investment ideas, co-managers Larry Auriana and Hans Utsch tripled their shareholders' investments from 1991 through 1995—a record that very few funds even came close to matching.

Yet contrary to the image this fund projects in its advertisements and in many press reports, Kaufmann is not a gunslinging fund that takes quick profits, that invests in teeny-tiny companies or that trades frenetically. Until 1995, in fact, Auriana, who turned 53 in 1996, and Utsch, 60, didn't even employ a trader. They entered the buy and sell orders themselves, just as they did all of their own investment research. The Auriana-Utsch approach is deceptively simple: Buy newly public companies with unique products—their term for this is "companies with a franchise"—and don't let go. The advantage that Auriana and Utsch hold is a track record on investing in initial public offerings that gives them instant access to the management of just about every company entering the stock market for the first time.

The result of this technique has been phenomenal. Kaufmann (named after its founder, from whom Auriana and Utsch bought the fund's investment adviser) returned 59% in 1988, 47% in 1989, 79% in 1991 and outperformed the overall market each of the next three years, too.

Late in 1995, we spoke with the duo in Kaufmann's offices near the Chrysler Building in midtown Manhattan to learn more about their investment methods as well as to air the concern of many investors: Was the fund, which had grown to $3 billion in assets, too big for the small-company field in which it trolls? In other words, was success turning it into something far different than when it began?

KIPLINGER'S: When you took over Kaufmann in 1986, had either of you ever managed money before?

AURIANA: No, but Hans and I had been analyzing small companies for decades.

UTSCH: The transition from analyzing to investing you sort of evolve into. There's no formula to follow, except that all of a sudden you'll find a stock and say, "My God, what a franchise! I want to own it," as opposed to, "Yeah, it's a nice story, but so what?"

That may be so, but your first full calendar year, 1987, was a disaster. How come the fund lost 37%?

UTSCH: We picked lousy stocks. Then, and now, we get most of our ideas from IPOs. We didn't have a big enough backlog of companies we had tracked to put into our portfolio.

AURIANA: And we had 20% of assets in one stock that fell from $10 to $2.50. That was devastating. We learned our lesson about diversifying.

When a prospectus of a company about to go public is plopped on your desk, what do you seek to learn from it?

UTSCH: From the prospectus, zero. We meet with five or six managements a day that are doing or just completed their IPOs. Often I'll read a prospectus the night before we meet with a company and say, "Why are we even having this meeting?" Then I listen to management and find that there is more to it.

AURIANA: If you had read the prospectus of HFS [formerly Hospitality Franchise Systems], which is our biggest holding today, you probably wouldn't have bought the stock.

UTSCH: You need to understand the value of a company's franchise—its unique ability. In the case of HFS, a franchisor and reservations system for hotels, you find out that there is almost no capital spending necessary, so that the enormous goodwill that is being amortized, plus the earnings, give the company free cash flow of gigantic proportions. When we understood that, we wanted every share of stock we could get our hands on.

How often do you "flip" an IPO—sell it immediately for a quick profit?

AURIANA: Almost never. There were a few instances recently when underwriters insisted we take some stock, even though we said we had no long-term interest in the company. One reason we get good allocations is that underwriters know we'll also be buying in the aftermarket.

Doesn't it cost a lot more to buy more shares of a stock after it goes public?

AURIANA: When HFS went public in December 1992, you could buy as many shares as you wanted in the aftermarket at the offering price. That's the kind of IPO market we like. A hot market for IPOs is not good for us.

Why not? Don't a great deal of Kaufmann's profits come from run-ups right after a stock goes public?

AURIANA: The initial allocation from the underwriter gets us started. But we're always buying shares later well in excess of what we were allocated in the IPO. The allocations are not an important element in our performance, which reflects the very substantial returns on companies we've owned a number of years.

Is there a rate of earnings growth you look for?

AURIANA: We prefer companies whose earnings can grow at least 20% a year.

Do valuations—things like price-earnings ratios—enter into your decision to buy or not to buy?

UTSCH: Usually not, except that in the past six months stocks have gone public at such big premiums—40, 50, 60 times earnings—that we've dropped out.

AURIANA: We don't have established targets for price or P/E ratios. If we did, I think that all of our biggest holdings today—the stocks that have done best for us—would have been sold long ago.

Viking Office Products, which we've owned since it went public in 1989 at $2.50, is $45 now. And believe me, it has never looked cheap and sometimes was excessively priced.

Are you "momentum" investors—buyers of stocks whose profits and prices are accelerating?

UTSCH: Absolutely not. We pray sometimes for down earnings because we might have a 200,000-share position in a stock and want a million shares but can't afford them.

Would you have invested in the IPO of Netscape? It went public at something like 45 times revenues, with no earnings.

UTSCH: No. We told the Morgan Stanley syndicate that we were not going to be an investor in the stock.

AURIANA: There have been a number of studies showing that over five years or so the average IPO underperforms the market, and I assume those studies are true. So this is an area of high risk. But our record proves that if your selection is good, you can very substantially outperform the market, and that's our game.

What are the key questions you ask a company?

UTSCH: What you're always worried about is gross margin [net sales minus the cost of goods sold]. We'll ask what's happening with gross margin because gross margin will tell you what's happening to pricing. If the gross margin doesn't get hit, or if it's hit for a good reason, such as spending more money on research and development, we're okay.

Aren't you also trying to assess the quality of management? How do you know you're dealing with competent, truthful managers?

UTSCH: That's why we very seldom buy an IPO that's not backed by an Alex. Brown & Sons or an even better underwriter.

AURIANA: You've got to hope the underwriter has done its job. The other check: Who was the venture capitalist behind the

company? We know that certain venture capitalists have really
screened companies they get behind.

**Most people never would have heard of 90% of the 300
companies you own. Yet the median market capitalization of
your portfolio keeps going up and up. Are you buying bigger
companies?**

AURIANA: Our average market capitalization is about $450
million. The value of companies in general keeps going up. When
Altera, our second-biggest holding, went public in 1988, it was a
microcap. Now it has well over $1 billion in market capitalization.
We've discovered about 20 companies like Altera—ones we really
believe in and in which we want to be long-term investors.

UTSCH: Market cap is not even a criteria when we buy a stock.
If it's a good company and we like it, we buy it.

AURIANA: The IPOs we invest in today have market caps of
$250 million to $1 billion. You won't find us buying companies worth
$50 million or $60 million.

Have you considered closing Kaufmann to new investors?

AURIANA: We think about it. If the size of the fund adversely
affected performance, we'd close down in a minute, because the only
thing we have to sell is good performance. We haven't seen that size
is affecting results. If it does, we'll close.

Size has advantages, too. Today when we want to meet the
managers of a company, we pick up the phone and get them in here. If
we call a top-rated analyst, our call gets returned. In 1988 we couldn't
get an audience with some analysts, and forget about managements.

**Most stocks you own are in health care, technology and
retailing. Is that by design?**

AURIANA: No. It just so happens that this is where the
companies come from.

UTSCH: But we do make sector calls. When we started buying
HFS, we looked at what is driving the hotel business, and we saw that

no new hotels had been built for years—no new money, no new growth. So next thing you know, we have four to six companies involved in the hotel industry because it's a great business to invest in—for the time being, anyway.

Your prospectus allows you to sell stocks short—to sell borrowed shares in hopes of buying them back later at a lower price. How do you pick stocks to sell short?
UTSCH: How? Very poorly!

Then why do you do it?
UTSCH: I'm not sure why.
AURIANA: Hans exaggerates. In 1995 we've lost money in shorts, but if you go back . . . .
UTSCH: We've lost money every year.
AURIANA: No, Hans, that's not true. Other years we've made money selling stocks short, even in years the market went up. But it's never a big deal with us.
UTSCH: But, look. With shorts you almost never make a 100% profit because the company goes bankrupt. If you're really good, you get a return of 50% or 60% on a short sale. That's if you're right. If you're wrong and the stock goes up, the sky is the limit to your losses.

Working almost side by side, do the two of you argue back and forth like this all day?
AURIANA: We have terrific disagreements, but I know that Hans's position is never personal. It is always objective. He'll change his mind in a minute, if he is convinced, and I'm the same way. But in the end, if one of us can't live with a stock, it's out, and there are no hard feelings.
UTSCH: We can disagree and both be right, too. Take a stock like Medisense. It sells meters that let diabetics measure the glucose level of their blood. Medisense all but gives the units away. But it sells these disposable strips that go in it, and that's where the money is—the same as with razor blades. So there's a huge revenue stream every time you place one of these meters. But meanwhile, there are

companies that are betting the ranch every day in R&D to come up with a noninvasive way of performing this same test. The person to come up with such a product will become a billionaire and Medisense will be out of business. Yet everybody who has tried to invent a noninvasive test has failed.

We've owned Medisense since it went public, and every time you see something in the newspaper about XYZ Co. testing a noninvasive process for testing blood, bam! the stock gets hit. That's going to continue, and every time Larry sees it happen he says, "Oh God! They're going out of business!" And I say, "Yeah, we've heard it all before."

AURIANA: I'm just saying this is a . . . .

UTSCH: So we argue about what to do and reduce our position a bit in the end. But Larry's right to want out of Medisense and I'm right to want to stay in it.

How long a time horizon should someone have to invest in Kaufmann?

AURIANA: Three to five years, minimum.

UTSCH: The only people who make money in stocks are the people who hold. You'll never see a trader go home rich. Never.

We've heard from a lot of readers who won't invest in Kaufmann because your expense ratio, 2.27%, is too high. Why don't you lower it? [At the time of the interview, the expense ration was 2.27%; it went to 2.17% in 1996.]

AURIANA: When we contemplated going into money management, the decision we had to make was to manage hedge-fund money or a public mutual fund. In a hedge fund, the manager gets 1% of assets per year for expenses and 20% of all the profits. We went with a public fund and manage it as we would a hedge fund.

UTSCH: The fee is irrelevant to the performance of this fund over a period of five or ten years. Now, if we were investing in AT&T, IBM and electric utilities, your readers would be absolutely right.

AURIANA: We invest in managements, not in numbers in a

prospectus, and the people who invest in this fund are getting its management, too—Hans and me. You're buying our lives. I don't think there's a fund like ours; we've followed small growth companies since the mid 1960s. We own the management company, so we're not going to quit and go to work for somebody else. We're here for the long term, and if you want to invest in us, that's the price you pay.

Besides, there has to be a price leader.

Unquestionably, size has affected Kaufmann fund. It started 1995 with $1.6 billion, ended the year with roughly twice as much, and roughly doubled in size in 1996. Where to invest the money? As always, a lot still went into new or recent IPOs. But a lot also goes into buying more shares of companies Kaufmann already owns, or into long-established stocks that Auriana and Utsch deem timely, such as Applied Materials, Cypress Semiconductors, Home Depot, LSI Logic and Micron Technology.

Result: Kaufmann is less of a pure IPO fund than it once was. For example, at the end of 1992, 34 of its 50 largest holdings had gone public in the previous 24 months. But as of mid 1995, only 21 of the top 50 fit that description. Kaufmann could continue to be an extraordinarily successful fund, but it will probably behave differently than it did when it owned primarily freshly minted stocks.

The year 1995 illustrates the effect of this shift away from new or recent IPOs. The fund loaded up on long-established semiconductor stocks early in 1995 and got hurt when prices of such stocks collapsed late in the year. But let's not cast stones. Kaufmann fund returned 37% in 1995, just a hair behind the scorching results of Standard & Poor's 500-stock index.

Alas, 1996 was another story altogether. Kaufmann shot out of the starting gate like a bullet. But it was caught by the mid-year crash of high-tech stocks and trailed the S&P 500 thereafter.

Robert Bacarella

I n 1974 Robert Bacarella, then a pension-fund manager for Borg-Warner Corp., and four friends began an investment club they named Monetta—Latin for money—with $750 in capital. The goal: Build it into a half-billion-dollar mutual fund. Monetta fund started on May 6, 1986, with $1.9 million in assets, substantially from the original investment club's coffers. The half-billion-dollar barrier was breached early in 1993, when Monetta closed its doors to new investors. (It has since reopened.)

Virtually all money managers follow disciplines that define their style. What distinguishes Bacarella, a lifelong Chicagoan born in 1949, is his ability to articulate how he chooses what to buy and what to sell. In fact, his critics might say he is almost a prisoner of his investment rules. Early on, those investment disciplines served him well. The fund dodged losses in the Crash year of 1987 and in the Kuwait war-inspired bear market year of 1990. And in 1991—a year made to order for a small-company growth fund—Monetta returned 56%.

The face of Bob Bacarella was on the cover of the March 1992 issue of *Kiplinger's Personal Finance Magazine,* and as editor of that cover story I've always felt bad about its impact. Assets of Monetta stood at $57 million at the end of 1991—and at $408 million a year later! The attention simply overwhelmed Bacarella—his family, too. They would spend weekends at their home addressing prospectuses requested the previous week, and have as many more dumped in the mailbox on Monday.

I suspected the flood of money lay behind Monetta's subsequent problems. In 1992, the fund returned a subpar 5%. And 1993 got off to a terrible start, raising red flags. It was in August of that year that I first interviewed Bacarella at Monetta's offices in Wheaton, Illinois. At the time, Bacarella resisted such suggestions.

KIPLINGER'S: Why did Monetta drop from among the top funds in total return to near the bottom?

BACARELLA: There's one reason: health care. We have 18% of our assets in health care stocks. Otherwise, our total return would very closely track the Nasdaq composite index.

Why maintain such a big weighting in a sector that investors are murdering?

It goes back to our style. We're somewhat contrarian in buying stocks.

Sure. You only buy stocks that go down!

We buy stocks that are down, with the view that things will improve.

Obviously, you have faith that the bloodletting in health-related stocks will cease.

Absolutely. What's happening is more related to politics than to fundamentals. The companies we own are doing fine. Their earnings are coming through. There have been very few disappointments. Right now the stocks remain depressed, but the worst is over. Things will begin to clear up when we get a little more direction from President Clinton.

Have your health care holdings remained the same all this time?

Some of the names have changed. We've shifted toward a higher quality of company and to companies that are somewhat insulated from price controls. HealthCare Compare, for instance, is a preferred-provider organization. People say, "If we go strictly to price controls, who needs a PPO?" What they forget is that HealthCare Compare has the premier management and cash to convert overnight to an HMO, should it choose to. But right now, why do it? Business is good. Enrollments continue to climb.

With the perfect clarity of hindsight, don't you wish you'd held back on all the health stocks?

No, because I'm going to be right. I just don't know the timing of it. Normally, when an industry falls out of favor it doesn't stay down longer than one or two quarters. Then it tends to bottom out and rise. But because of what happened on the political front, and all the uncertainty, this is an unusual period. In fact, I think this is probably the best time to buy health care stocks.

What keeps you chipper when even your dog hates you?

I've had periods like this before and always come through them. In the third quarter of '89, Monetta was down 20%. Right now I'm down 6% for the year. I can make that up with any uptick in health care. [Monetta's total return for 1993: 0.5%.]

Have your methods of selecting stocks changed in the past year?

No, and in fact we follow very rigid disciplines. The start of our selection process is to screen a computer data base. There are certain parameters we want to see. We want a high return on equity—at least 20%. We want a pretax profit margin above 10% and a debt-to-equity ratio of less than 50%. We're looking for earnings momentum. By that, I want to see the rate of earnings growth improve perhaps 5% per quarter. I want low volatility if I can find it, but you have to live with a lot of volatility in the emerging-growth area.

What size company do you focus on?

We average $500 million in market value, in a range of $50 million to $2 billion. I've upped the maximum in the past year, from $1 billion. With technology stocks, you have to stretch the maximum a little bit to pick them up.

How many candidates will your screens identify?

From 200 to 250. Then we do our basic valuation work. Let's take an example of a company we think is going to earn $1 a share

in the next 12 months and whose growth rate is 30%. We know historically that in a bull market investors are willing to pay a price-
earnings ratio equal to the annual rate of earnings growth. So on
the high end the company is worth $30. But in a bear market that
same company might sell for only half its growth rate. That's $15.
The midpoint is $22. Then we apply our market-sentiment
indicators.

What indicators do you look at?

Such things as the percent of cash in mutual funds, the number
of advisory services that are bearish and the ratio of buys to sells
among corporate insiders. There are ten indicators in all, and the
two readings we take of each—six months previous, and current—
give you a flavor for what people are feeling. We started this system
in 1985, and it has been very good over time in forecasting what will
happen in the next six months.

So today, with the market setting a new all-time record, what do the indicators tell you?

The indicators tell us that this is not the time to be overly
aggressive in buying stocks. Take mutual fund cash levels. When
cash levels are between 8% and 12% of assets, that's neutral and we
assign a zero; above 12% is a plus, below 8% a minus. [The level at
that time was 10%, or neutral.]

We do this for all ten indicators. We add the pluses and minuses
and come up with the index number. A reading of 200 would be
neutral. The lowest number—155—came in August 1987, just
before the crash. In January 1988, it was the highest—255. The
index is now at 185. That implies the risk of a 5% or 10% market
correction.

How do you use these indicators?

Taking my example again, you multiply the percentage of
indicators that are positive by the $30 bull-market price, the
percentage that are negative by the $15 bear-market price and the

percentage that are neutral by the $22 midpoint price. When you add those together, you get a target price. If a stock is selling 30% or more below the target, then I can buy it with some confidence.

Okay, you've bought the stock. When do you sell it?

On the upside, when it goes up 30%. Then we don't buy it back for at least 30 days.

Why 30%? Why not 100%?

I admit I don't know when to sell. I cannot pick a top. But I know that, historically, stocks move in 30% increments. So if you can find the base, you'll notice a stock goes up 30% and rests. Very rarely will it go straight up. We hope to make our 30% in a year. But if a stock goes up 30% in two days, we're out.

This also goes to the old saying, "Never fall in love with your stocks." One of the biggest problems portfolio managers have is that they get emotionally attached to stocks they've chosen and they don't want to sell. "Hey, I'm sticking with my winners!" How often have you heard people say that? Whatever sell discipline they once had gets pushed aside.

But why get rid of your best-performing stocks?

The nature of small growth companies is that when they do well, they start expanding inventory, building new plants, adding new employees. What happens to quarterly earnings gains? They go down. There's nothing wrong with that; they have to go through these costs of putting new capital into the business. So the earnings momentum isn't going to be there all the time. And then what happens? A 1-cent shortfall and the stock gets zapped. That's your entry point to buy again. We will play the same stock over and over again. DSC Communications—the old Digital Switch—is our biggest holding today. We got into that stock for the first time a long time ago. Now we're sellers because it went up 30% again.

How far down will you ride a losing stock?

Ideally we want to cap a loss at 30%, too. But our system is more complex than that. We track our holdings every day. We're always looking at each stock's price movement relative to the rest of its industry and to the market. So when a technology stock goes down 10% and the other technology stocks go up, we know something's out of whack. If the trend continues for five trading days, the stock is telling us that somebody, somewhere knows more than we do. We'll call management, although that seldom helps—they'll usually say they can't explain what's happening. Then my trading department calls around to traders and analysts. Who's hitting the stock, why is it down when its industry is up, and so forth.

If a stock goes down 20%, we're seriously concerned. But I might add to my position.

Your cash position today is 17%. Will it stay there?

It depends upon the values. I don't set a cash position. It's a function of the process I just described. If I find things I can make 30% on in the next year, I'll put all my money to work today.

You recently started a new fund, Monetta Midcap. How much of your time do you spend on it?

Zero. I just run Monetta.

In retrospect, should you have closed Monetta to new investors earlier?

I don't think the performance was affected by asset size. The money came in at a steady pace. If anything, it helped future performance by letting us increase our positions and average down our costs. If you go back to day one, with the investment club, our goal was always to get to $500 million. We just got there sooner than I thought.

Monetta fund perked up in 1995, ultimately returning 28% to the S&P 500's 38%. A good part of the year it led the index. The fund still held a big position in health care stocks—just different names. Now

Bacarella focused on "medical labor unions"—what he calls companies that are essentially doctor-controlled businesses set up to negotiate rates with HMOs and patients.

In 1996, Bacarella owned up to the problem he wouldn't acknowledge in 1993—dealing with the octupling of his fund's asset base in 1992 and into 1993. In a rapidly rising market, having more money to invest each and every day is a blessing. In a flat or waffling market—such as 1992, when the S&P 500 index returned 7.6% in 1992—it could be a curse.

I asked Bacarella if he had reconsidered and altered his investment methods after four straight years of underperforming the S&P index. No, he replied, the rules he invests by hadn't changed. "You have to know why you went astray," he said. "Where we went wrong was in not having in place an infrastructure to follow the stocks we were putting into the portfolio." What he means is that the number of stocks owned by Monetta jumped from 40 to 110 rather quickly, and with Bacarella and his family stuffing envelopes with prospectuses every night, his attention was distracted. Instead of acting only on his own research, Bacarella relied on recommendations of brokerage-firm analysts. These analysts may have liked or disliked specific stocks for good reasons, but those weren't necessarily Bacarella's reasons, and "this set us back a ways."

Echoes of Ralph Wanger (see page 156). The curse of managers of small-company funds is that there's not an inexhaustible supply of good companies to invest in. A law of inverse rewards is at work: The more money you make, the more pours in; the bigger your pot of money, the less you can target the small companies that generated the great returns in the first place. You either buy dangerously high levels of shares in these companies, settle for second-best or third-best alternatives, or build up your level of cash. Good managers like Bacarella and Wanger do the right thing—close their funds to new investors. It's just that Bacarella didn't close Monetta soon enough.

But there's more going on with Monetta than just asset growth.

For all Bacarella's efforts from 1992 through 1996, nothing seemed to lift the fund out of its rut. I suspect the problem lies in Bacarella's investing methodology. It was devised in one era, the second half of the 1980s, but didn't translate well into the markets of the 1990s. For instance, the rule of selling every stock when it rises 30% is pure hokum. (Bacarella dropped that requirement in 1996.)

The lesson is this: While undisciplined investing doesn't work, neither does a highly disciplined system that is divorced from reality.

Elizabeth Bramwell

On Wall Street, the name Gabelli stands for old-fashioned value investing of the sort practiced with celebrated success by Mario Gabelli since the 1970s (page 11). So it might surprise you to learn that the person who for some years ran the most celebrated Gabelli fund was not the master himself. Nor was it a fund dedicated to undervalued securities. No. The fund was Gabelli Growth, and the manager was Elizabeth Bramwell. She and Gabelli met as students at Columbia Graduate School of Business in the late 1960s. After Gabelli formed his own investment company, Bramwell became its director of research. And when Gabelli began launching funds a decade later, Bramwell started the second one, oriented toward growth, in early 1987.

Some fund it was. In 1988, '89, '90 and yet again in '91, Gabelli Growth beat both Gabelli Asset—Mario's flagship fund—and Standard & Poor's 500-stock index in total return. Alas, that string of successes was broken in 1992. When I visited Bramwell (who has since left to form her own fund, as discussed beginning on page 93) in her cluttered Manhattan office late that year, the purpose was to explore the methods of a disciplined growth-stock investor, in good times and bad.

KIPLINGER'S: The year 1992 will be the first year your fund didn't beat the overall market. What didn't click?

BRAMWELL: In 1991 a lot of stocks in the portfolio spiked in December, hitting all-time highs. Then the first half of 1992 was kind of cruel.

You started 1992 with a lot of health care stocks that got sick, right?

Yes. The biotechs in 1991's fourth quarter really swept this fund upward. Then they gave it back in the first half of '92. Now they're rebounding. At the moment we're about 15% invested in the health field.

What stocks were you buying at the peak that sank out of sight?

I think the argument is more, should one have traded out of stocks like Johnson & Johnson when it ended 1991 at $57, or 20 times what I expect it to earn in 1993? I try to be early owning a stock. And I caused myself a problem early in 1992 by using my 1993 earnings estimates to figure price-earnings ratios. So maybe I was too early. But in the long run, you want to be in good stocks early rather than not at all. Stocks don't move up in straight lines.

Is there a strong temptation to switch horses—to shake up the portfolio—when the stocks you like languish?

In the long run—which is what I run this fund for—I think that fundamental analysis of earnings for the next year and couple of years beyond that is the way to go. And my methodology for finding good stocks doesn't change, although it does get refined.

Speaking of stocks, the ones owned by Gabelli Growth defy easy analysis. What, for instance, do a Johnson & Johnson and an Illinois Tool Works have in common?

In each instance, you've got companies that are run for the long term. They've got a lot of bets—not just one. J&J is a classic growth company, with a huge pipeline of new products coming along. Ditto Illinois Tool Works. It's a well-managed company with a long-term commitment to its business. Its culture is that of a small company that customizes its products. Yet it is one of the largest fastener companies in the world. Its products were used in the new English Channel tunnel and in the new pyramid outside the Louvre.

Your portfolio turnover is quite low—50% to 60% a year. What accounts for that?

I'm not focused on trading stocks. I buy and anticipate holding for some 18 months. One plus is that it's tax-efficient for the shareholders.

Some successful fund managers ignore what's going on around them—the "big picture" in the economy. Do you fit that mold?

The big picture is important. I look closely at economic, political and tax developments. In fact, some of the gains of the fund came from major macro decisions. I thought the market was too expensive in August of 1987, and by the end of September I had one-third of assets in cash. Meanwhile, I was watching the House Ways and Means Committee when it proposed to eliminate the deductibility of interest expenses in mergers and acquisitions. That would have lowered the value of entire companies by increasing carrying costs. By Black Monday I was 41% in cash.

After the crash, the fundamentals of the economy still looked terrific. A lot of newly public companies, like A&W Brands, really got hit because they were extremely new. So the fund benefited from having cash to buy such stocks at their lows late in '87.

The fund was extremely new, too, wasn't it?

Yes, and the lucky part was that I wasn't given $100 million to invest the first day. Assets at the end of '87 were only $3.6 million. They didn't hit $25 million until 1989.

What other major assumptions have you made at the fund?

The next big macro theme was "Europe '92." Tariffs were going to come down and specifications would become uniform and it would be easier to do business and consolidate plants in Europe. It was a big play, and it worked. Then the Berlin Wall came down, the Soviet satellites broke away and markets around the world opened up that nobody thought would.

So where are we now on macro themes? I think inflation will be relatively modest because you have free movement of capital and people, plus overcapacity in the world. Interest rates should hold steady, so we'll have gradual rather than hurried growth.

I'm optimistic about the stock market. It won't be like the 1980s, which was instant gratification. But the '90s should be a 10%-a-year decade for stocks, with the potential for more. We're in the last decade of the millennium. The 1790s were a great period for the development of constitutional government and democracy. The 1890s were a great period for invention, discovery and industry. The 1990s will get a little bit of all of this. There's a positive thrust just by living in the last decade of a millennium.

How do you go about analyzing stocks?

I look at earnings and earnings-growth rates. Right now, at the end of 1992, I am working from earnings estimates for the end of 1993 and even mid 1994. As I said, I think it pays to own a stock early. The theme I'm working on now is that by mid 1993 investment payoffs will start to fall into place. For example, a lot of global companies have been building plants and marketing staffs in nations like Hungary or Thailand or India or China, and you'll see some payoffs beginning in 1994. Procter & Gamble in 1985 had 28% of sales outside the U.S. Now it's up to about 48%. But overseas earnings aren't up to 48% of total profits, so you have a potential "kicker" that could accelerate earnings.

When you find a stock you like, how do you decide whether it's overpriced? When is a high price-earnings ratio too high?

As an example, I've trimmed my Coca-Cola holdings. Coke traded at 25 times my 1993 earnings estimate. The earnings-growth rate had been about 20% a year, but I think it's coming down, to maybe 17%. I thought that a P/E of 25 for a company growing at 17% a year was high, even for Coke. A P/E equal to the growth rate, based on 1993 earnings, is my general threshold.

The fund owns Wal-Mart Stores and Home Depot, which trade at P/Es far higher than their growth rates. Why not sell?

The P/Es of both stocks are about 1.5 times their growth rates on 1993 earnings. My argument for not selling is that both are gaining market share and have tremendous financial clout. Their managements appear to be pretty lean and hungry—pretty entrepreneurial.

So a P/E ratio of 1.5 times the growth rate is not always a sell signal, as with Coke.

It depends in part on your other opportunities at the moment. Besides, these two companies could accelerate their earnings as the economy picks up. Why mess around with other stocks? Let these keep doing the work.

It always amazes us where portfolio managers get ideas. Do some of yours come out of personal experiences?

I'm a big believer in finding ideas by looking around you. For example, my children's friends have been spontaneously switching from Coke to fruit juices. Then you find out that the macho people on First Boston's trading floor are drinking more fruit juice, and the same seems true at social gatherings. And I own Northern Trust because of its global stock-custody work—a growing area I became more aware of because of this fund's future needs.

One reason I own Biogen, which makes the hepatitis B vaccine and earns royalties from it, is that when I took my children for physicals last June it was strongly recommended that they be vaccinated. You get not just one shot but three, staggered. Sure enough, the stock has strengthened in the past six months.

And the tip-off to you was from taking your kids to the doctor?
Right. You have to look at events in life a little bit differently.

Do your fund and Mario's Gabelli Asset fund converge in any way?
The main thing that's common is our emphasis on primary research. I really don't use Mario for ideas. This fund is oriented toward forecasting future earnings. It looks at companies at the beginning of their life cycles rather than at the end. I don't want to speak for Mario, but in Gabelli Asset you're looking more at historical ratios to find undervalued companies.

Do you have carte blanche with Gabelli Growth? Does

Gabelli ever veto your picks?

Yes, I do, and no, he doesn't. Mario wasn't even on Gabelli Growth's board of trustees for the first five years.

If you were retired and living in Arizona, where would you be getting your ideas?

I think I'd buy mutual funds. You can move around in the fund universe, too. Actually, I'd probably have a Quotron and sit there with humongous files on stocks cluttering my retirement home!

Thirteen months after the above interview, Elizabeth Bramwell resigned to begin her own fund—appropriately enough called Bramwell Growth. Litigation between her and ex-employer Mario Gabelli over what she was owed obscured an interesting fact: For virtually all of 1994, Gabelli Growth was run by Mario himself, who epitomizes the opposite of an earnings-growth investor. Nothing extraordinary occurred. Most long-term-growth funds had slightly negative total returns that year. So did Gabelli Growth.

On August 1, 1994, six months after leaving Gabelli Growth, Elizabeth Bramwell had Bramwell Growth up and running. During the next 18 months its return pretty much matched that of the S&P 500—no mean feat, considering that very few other funds could do as well without plunging head-first into the technology sector, which Bramwell Growth did not.

When I spoke to her early in 1996, Bramwell owned a lot of the stocks in her new fund that she had nourished in Gabelli Growth—issues like Illinois Tool Works, Procter & Gamble and Johnson & Johnson. But Wal-Mart Stores and Home Depot—two of the classic growth stocks of the prior decade and staples of Gabelli Growth a few years earlier—had disappeared. Both stocks shot up until their price-earnings ratios exceeded one-and-a-half times their rates of earnings growth, and were sold. "That's what we're talking about now with Coca-Cola," she said. "Coke's growth rate is 17 to 18% a year and it sells at about 28 times earnings. Coke is a great company—I still own a few shares—but there are better opportunities."

Among the differences between Gabelli Growth and Bramwell Growth is assets—the former had $700 million when she left, and the latter had one-fourth as much in 1996, "which means in theory that I have more agility." Bramwell's investing methods remained the same, she said—a top-down overlay of investment themes and a bottom-up emphasis on earnings growth at a reasonable price-earnings ratio. The globalization of U.S. business remained a theme. Other themes in 1996: companies that own intellectual property— copyrighted songs, for instance, in the case of Gaylord Entertainment—and companies in the fastest-growth region of the U.S., the Pacific Northwest.

I asked Bramwell if she is usually confident of the correctness of her investment decisions. "I tell my kids," she replied, "that this is a business about changing your mind. I do it on all 85 or 90 stocks we own. I think about them all, every day—adding to some, subtracting from others. You have to be flexible." That's true, and it's a pity that 1996 ultimately disappointed Bramwell's investors. The fund trailed the S&P 500 substantially. *Morningstar Mutual Funds* blamed her fund's heavy weighting in tech stocks. Or maybe she simply followed the wrong trends or picked false beneficiaries of those trends.

James Craig

J ames Craig hadn't quite turned 30 when he took over Janus
fund in 1986 from founder Tom Bailey. In each of the next five
calendar years, Janus delivered above-average total returns
among long-term-growth funds, with below-average volatility.
The money poured in. In fact, in the first half of the 1990s no single
money manager attracted money faster than this unassuming
Alabamian. As recently as 1989, Janus was just one among many
growth funds and had less than $400 million in assets. By late 1993, at
the time this first interview took place, assets had grown by a factor
of 25, to more than $9 billion, and by late 1996 approached $20 billion.

That's a lot of money. And it goes to a question that haunts money
managers everywhere: At what point does the growth in assets
become self-defeating by making it impossible for the manager to
employ the very methods that created success in the first place? Craig
built his reputation on two great years, 1989 (when assets ended the
year at $705 million) and 1991 ($3 billion). Since then the money has
kept coming in, but the results have been only average. So what's the
matter? Is it the nature of the stock market in the years since 1989?
Something Craig is not doing that he once did? Or is it just that
damned money? We explored those issues, as well as Craig's
investment methods, one sunny afternoon in late 1993 in Denver.

**KIPLINGER'S: Janus fund has elements of growth and value
in it. Which of those styles best describes your approach?**

CRAIG: Stock prices move on earnings. I'm an earnings-growth
investor. I will go anywhere and buy anything to get that—whether
it's an auto company or a biotech company. I'm looking for earnings
acceleration beyond what Wall Street generally expects. So in some
cases I'll buy railroads, which you wouldn't consider growth stocks.
But I find that if the pattern of earnings is changing, generally Wall
Street is way behind. By pattern of earnings, I mean that a company's

cost structure changes, and its earnings react more favorably than expected to changes in the economy.

You're not interested in quality of management and all that?

Oh, definitely we are. We meet practically all of the managements whose stocks we own—they're the ones who make it tick. But basically, we analyze the financial numbers. We spend most of our time modeling the earnings and we pester the hell out of companies to make sure our models are really getting at the trends. Sometimes we do a better job at estimating the earnings than the companies do.

Where do you get ideas for stock purchases?

Most come from looking at quarterly earnings reports—400 a day during those couple of weeks four times a year. It's just crazy. That's where you see data points that tell you there's been a change in the trend. Other ideas come from reading the tape [news services]. In fact, the biggest move I've made in Janus fund recently was to rebuy Wal-Mart stock, based on information coming across the tape that signaled a consolidation of its industry. Pace sold virtually all its stores to Wal-Mart. Costco Wholesale and Price Club merged in October. BJ's Wholesale is reporting losses.

The discounting industry is consolidating into two players per market, and in many markets just one—Wal-Mart. Meanwhile, Wall Street has taken a disliking to the discounting industry. So we undertook to rebuild our position in Wal-Mart.

It's not like we know anything that other people don't know. But still, I expect that by spring or summer of 1994 the wholesale-club business will be liked by Wall Street and that Wal-Mart will be in the mid to upper $30s.

You acted like a contrarian investor, didn't you?

A lot of earnings-momentum people jump into companies with strong earnings growth regardless of the price-earnings multiple. In this market, they're doing very well. I tend not to do great when technology stocks are hot, as now, because I have some idea of what a business should be worth. I determine basically that when P/E equals the long-term growth rate of the business, I'll sell the stock. My experience is that the market always comes back to that guideline.

Now, I could be totally wrong. We may get into an environment in the 1990s, with interest rates down so low, that people value companies at two times the earnings-growth rate. I'm going to have a lot of problems adjusting to that. But as it stands now, I don't really care about the stock's technical behavior or its momentum. I'm just looking for situations in which Wall Street just hasn't caught on to a change in an earnings trend.

Nothing glamorous about that.

No, there's no macrotheory, no glamorous vision.

Can you cite an example of a recent stock purchase where you saw something in the quarterly earnings that led you to buy the stock?

I guess the biggest move recently would be in Switzerland, with Roche. It's in an industry I do not like. In fact, this is my only health care stock. Roche had four divisions, three of which were very inferior to their peers in terms of returns. So they reorganized the company and improved the operations to give a big push to the bottom line—it's just that simple. Sales in 1992 were up 13%, earnings 29%.

How did you research that stock?

First, I called Roche in Switzerland. Their English is a lot better than my French. Management told us the steps that were taken, the results they expected and the time they expected it would take to achieve those results. Anyone could have called the company in Switzerland and gotten the same response.

We got all the brokerage research on Roche that we could find, to learn what the expectations were for it. Then we put our own numbers into an earnings model on a spreadsheet and found a difference between our expectations for this stock and those of everyone else. When we find that difference, we get really aggressive.

Are you having difficulty finding those big differences in expectations?

At certain times, such as now, Wall Street already has high expectations. It's hard for us to find "added value." The U.S. market is totally picked over. Whenever you have this size of a market move, the amount of money involved is huge, and the amount of research going into finding an undervalued situation is immense. This has been going on for three years, and it is very hard to find any unknown or undiscovered trend to invest in.

Now you're talking like a value investor.

Yes, that's what happens, and a lot of people get real freaked out by it. My attitude may be based on my southern conservatism—or just working for Tom Bailey all these years. If you miss opportunities on the upside, that's not good—you have to perform. But doing worse than average in a down market can put you out of business. Most people my age have no clue what a long, vicious bear market is like. If I lose people's money, they won't care that the overall market was down 35% and I was down only 28%. I talked to a doctor whose losses in the '87 crash extended the time he would have to work by two years. Of course, he pulled his money out at the wrong time, when he was down 20%. Our shareholders have kids to put through college and plans for retirement. Take somebody's capital down 20% or 30% and you've really impaired his lifestyle. You lose his business.

What's your cash position now?

About 25%. It has been as high as 50%, in July and August of 1990, at the time of Iraq's invasion of Kuwait. I was invested in a lot of companies that didn't make the profits I expected. As it turned out, the reason was that the economy was going into a recession. We missed numbers all over the place. I sold those stocks immediately. I was creamed.

The cash level is a residual of my stock decisions. I don't know why, but I always end up, on average, with 15% to 25% of assets in cash. To me, that's still enough exposure to stocks to lose you a lot of money. I mean, people talk about 20% cash as being an insurance policy against a market decline. That's absolutely not true. It's the stocks you own—not your cash position—that matter. In some portfolios, you could be 50% in cash and still be killed by a bear market.

Do you make any assumptions at all about the economy or the stock market?

We pay close attention to the economy, basically by talking to businesses.

You know, predicting the future is impossible. What I try to do with the economy is just note that businesses are doing well or not doing well. In July of 1990 I determined that the economy was slowing, big time.

The way I approach it is to assume that when the market is at a peak, I'll find little opportunity out there. I'll have my highest cash position at the top of a market.

You said that you sell a stock when its P/E ratio equals its rate of earnings growth. When are you a buyer?

An attractive valuation to me would be when we calculate that a company's earnings for the next three years should grow at a rate of 20%, and its stock sells for 15 times earnings for the 12 months starting about six months from now. I can make money off a P/E ratio like that. Even if the P/E stays the same, the stock rises with the earnings. But if the earnings are growing at a 20% rate and the P/E ratio is already 19, I'm not that interested.

Is it fair to say that every successful fund manager has a set of rules—a discipline—that he or she adheres to?

I've never known anyone who did well in this business by

changing his discipline to fit the market. I've known people who
didn't do well because they had rules that were too rigid. I mean,
you could have a strict rule to buy a stock only when its P/E gets
below 8 and its yield is above 4%. It may work, but not for very long
and not consistently. What works for me is to fantasize that I'm
buying into businesses that will do better than is generally
expected.

And I have to avoid casting aside that discipline and buying
stocks just because they're hot.

A bit like resisting the devil?

Yes, but look at the consequences. We have 800,000
shareholders, and if we get phone calls from half of 1% complaining
that we're doing badly, we're flooded. I was talking recently to a
friend of my wife's, at a time when I was ahead of the market. But
because Fidelity's funds were just smoking from big gains, the guy
says to me, "How does it feel to be having such a bad year?" And I
just went ballistic. But now I see his point. If your team's pitcher gets
out there and walks four batters instead of his normal one, you beat
on him. It's human psychology.

So the temptation is to do things a little bit differently sometimes?

Oh, the temptation is tremendous. I see what's working—which
stocks are going up, and why. It's so hard to resist buying.

Why resist? Why not buy, and when whatever propels the stock upward stops propelling it, sell?

What generally happens to me if I break my discipline is that I
don't know when to sell. It's just like buying off a hot tip from a
broker. If I don't know why I own it, then I have absolutely no idea
what I'm doing. I might just as well be speculating.

Because of the way the market has behaved the past year or two—one record after another—do you ever

wonder whether your rules of what a stock is worth don't apply anymore?

No. One thing is never different: Businesses without a strong franchise and overvalued businesses eventually do very poorly.

Janus fund had a great 1991—up 43%. What happened after that?

Since then, we've matched the market—nothing to make anyone really happy. Why? I'm the world's worst technology investor. I'm thoroughly convinced that there is no franchise to those businesses. Product cycles are so fast that it's very difficult for them to make money. There's no barrier to new competitors—a couple of engineers in their garage can make a supercomputer. Even IBM has finally fallen. They all will.

But lately the stocks of small technology companies are going wild. I owned Cisco Systems in July of '91 and made a 45% profit. I reached my target and I sold it. Since then it has tripled and now has a $6-billion market capitalization. But I have a hard time owning a stock unless I can believe in the strength of its business into the future.

We're not going to swing for the outside pitch. If you run money like that, you're going to have accidents. If I can incur less volatility to achieve the fund's return, I'd like to do that. Other funds run differently, and their products are perfect for other people. If my family or friends think the stock market's great and want to max out, I send them to Kansas City [Twentieth Century funds]. Those guys are 100% in the hot stuff, and if the market's good they are going to smoke.

How many stocks does Janus hold now?

Sixty-eight. It's an awfully concentrated portfolio for a $9-billion fund, and it reflects the fact that I buy only stocks I believe in—stocks I can go to war for.

What would it take for Janus to have another 50% year?

It would take a lot of Wal-Marts and Home Depots—good-quality companies—having significant climbs in share price with no deterioration in the fundamentals. Or knock a thousand points off the Dow Jones industrial average.

What should your investors expect for the future, long term?
We should be able to compound money consistently. I have a lot of flexibility and I'm waiting for my shot. Every two or three years, I have a big year. And then the other two I moan and gripe and cuss and stress out because I can't seem to get an edge.

––––––––––––––––

More than two years later, Craig was still waiting for his edge. "I need a big year," he acknowledged when we spoke at the end of 1995. "I'm paid on performance, and I haven't had a bonus since 1991. I need to put up some returns significantly better than the S&P 500's." It didn't happen in 1995, in part because, as in 1993, technology stocks were on a tear but lacked the predictability of earnings that is the touchstone of Craig's investing technique.

But the stock market's advance in 1995 caused Craig to bend some investment rules. He spoke in 1993 of buying a stock at a significantly lower price-earnings ratio than its rate of expected earnings growth, and selling when the two numbers were equal. "Interest rates are the key variable. With rates down at these levels, I have to be flexible. I sold one-third of Janus's Merck stock at $58, following my rule. But I held the rest and the stock went to $67 because the stability of its earnings growth at these rates of interest makes the stock still attractive." In other words, stock values may be getting pricier, but there's no better alternative for investors to turn to.

Roche remained in the portfolio—in fact, it was the fourth-largest holding going into 1996. But other ideas hadn't worked out— Wal-Mart, for instance. "The stock had gone from $35 to $25 when we bought it, and I thought it would turn around when the industry consolidated. But that did not happen. To reinvigorate its earnings, Wal-Mart had to reinvigorate its Sam's Club stores, but instead it downsized them to appeal to small businesses! We got out at about the price we got in, but we lost a year with our money."

That's part of the Craig approach: When something doesn't work as you expected, don't become stubborn; go on to a better idea instead. "I've watched people hold on after the reason they owned the stock evaporated," he said, "and it's just disastrous." A good example of this was the stocks of paper companies in 1995. Craig was a buyer because the industry had succeeded in making nine successive price increases stick and wasn't adding capacity. So it looked as if earnings would be predictable, and handsome. "It turned out that the companies could squeeze a lot more production out of their existing plants—they call it 'de-bottlenecking,'" said Craig. "Plus we got hit with a slowing economy. So guess what? That business will not stabilize, as we had thought. We sold our positions."

As to the fund's manageability with those billions of assets, Craig could only say: "I'll know I've got too much money when I get there. I just don't know where 'there' is. The market has expanded its capitalization in line with my fund's growth in assets. I can't make a small railroad like Wisconsin Central my biggest position, as I did when I ran Janus Venture. But with a big holding like Electronic Data Services, owning 10 million shares is not that big a deal." At any rate, Janus went into the last quarter of 1996 well ahead of the S&P 500; maybe Jim would finally get his bonus.

Shelby Davis

An academician I once interviewed claimed it would take as many as 80 years of data to prove statistically that a money manager's market-beating performance was due to superior talent rather than dumb luck. Shelby Davis won't run a fund that long, but here's a statistic that will make you not want to wait 80 years: During 20 of the 27 years that he has managed Davis New York Venture fund, Shelby Davis has outperformed Standard & Poor's 500-stock index. Nobody else running a fund today can say as much. Result: a total return during the past two decades that's half again as great as the S&P's.

How Davis achieved that record was the subject of our interview in New York City in the summer of 1993. And it became clear that some pretty simple, common-sense investment methods, and not luck, account for his results. Davis, born in 1937, is a patient man, as befits someone who has run the same fund for more than a quarter century. He likes to buy the stocks of growing companies when they've been bloodied by bad news and hold them as they return to favor and then some. Portfolio turnover is modest. He has particular affection for the stocks of banks, thrifts, brokerages and insurance companies—businesses he thinks are in growth industries of the 1990s and beyond.

KIPLINGER'S: Davis New York Venture is a fund that seems to thrive in any climate. What are you doing that everyone else isn't?

DAVIS: We strive for consistency by straddling different investment styles. We're eclectic. But one thing that helps in this day of herd mentality is to take out some of the risk by buying a stock that has already been killed. I like to find stocks that are beaten down in price so I can enter at a deflated level. What I'm looking for is growth at a reasonable price.

What's a "reasonable" price?

I'm willing to accept a price-earnings ratio that's equal to the growth rate in earnings. However, the higher the growth rate the less I'm willing to pay for the stock because the less sustainable I think the growth will be. When I get to a 20% grower, I'll rarely buy it for 20 times earnings.

I'm also looking for the potential for some positive change that will bring the price back up. And I want the company that I'm buying to fit within a conceptual framework that makes sense to me.

What stock fits that description now?

A classic example is Student Loan Marketing Association—Sallie Mae. Bill Clinton wants to put it out of business. His announcement triggered a decline in the stock price, from $73 to $42 per share. We had looked at Sallie Mae but always thought that the price-earnings multiple was too high, considering the company's growth rate. When it crashed, we started buying. The earnings estimates for this year are close to $5 a share. So at $42 it sold for about eight times earnings. It has a huge return on equity and a steady growth rate in earnings, in the range of 15% a year.

The student-loan program is going to double in size. The question is, who will get the business—the government, directly through the Department of Education, or the banks, whose loans will be sold to Sallie Mae? I don't really relish political risk, but I hope common sense will overtake political considerations. The prospect of the Department of Education running a new program making three or four million direct loans per year, with the complexities and paperwork and inefficiencies of both the government and the schools, is crazy.

Sallie Mae is a good buy. Even if the worst happens, it will take more than a decade to run out of existing student loans.

Have you set a target price for getting out of Sallie Mae?

I'm not one for setting a target for selling. I like to think that we buy stocks when they're at a pressure point, and that we buy at a price we can live with for a long time. Then we get a bonus when the price recovers to its normal level. Finally, we keep the stock and achieve growth in line with the company's higher earnings. Sallie Mae at $65 would still be selling at less than 12 times projected 1994 earnings. With earnings growth of 12% to 15% as far as the eye can see, the growth in the stock price from $65 on should at least match the growth in earnings. I like to buy at a value price, but I really want to end up with a growth company.

I'm comfortable owning companies over two or three recessions or market cycles because I get to know them better. When a bear market occurs or a bad quarter hits a company I like, I get a chance to add to a position at a bargain price. And I may do so over and over again.

But surely you have some rules of thumb for when a stock is overpriced . . . .

A profit margin that appears unsustainable is a signal to look carefully. The other warning sign is when the P/E ratio gets well above the earnings-growth rate.

I tend to sell a position gradually. Maybe it's because you never know when to say when. But I'll tell you what haunts me: I believe that this decade will be like the 1960s was for investors, and I remember looking back at that decade in 1970 and asking myself, "Why did I spend time on anything but growth stocks?" Wall Street back then was littered with the bones of investors who sold Polaroid and Xerox and Avon—the growth stocks of that day—too soon.

Are you saying, why sell stocks that are doing well for you, even if they do look overvalued?

Right. In the 1960s the big growth stocks—the Nifty 50, they were called—got bid up to 40 times earnings. The time to worry about this market is after we've gone through a similar period of euphoria.

Which raises a question: Do you pay attention to the market in making investments?

Every portfolio manager pays attention to it. But I try to focus on what is knowable and important rather than what's unknowable and important. What's unknowable and important is the market's next direction. What's knowable is that we've been in hog heaven for a decade. Yields are low, P/E multiples are high. Fortunately, we're at the bottom of a profit cycle. Fortunately, the alternatives don't look so attractive. And fortunately, the focus has been on certain stocks, so a whole lot of other companies can get in the spotlight before we bring down the curtain on the bull market. I'm referring to cyclical companies and financial stocks and a lot of mid-cap and small companies, and eventually a final run at the growth companies again.

You don't sound pessimistic.

To focus on the short term would be grossly myopic. Suppose, for instance, that we're at the start of an economic recovery. The typical recovery lasts 60 to 80 months. That's the rest of this decade. Also suppose our economic recovery is followed by one in England and then Germany and the rest of Europe. Then South America kicks in, and Asia keeps rolling and growing. Suddenly, you may start to see a glow of euphoria around the world. P/E ratios will be justified at higher and higher numbers. You'll begin seeing stories about the "great economic miracle of the Western World." Then is when you should become worried.

Getting back to the here and now for a moment, more than one-third of your portfolio is in financial stocks. What's going on?

The trick to buying a growth company cheap is to buy when other investors haven't recognized that it is in a growth industry. I think the entire investment-banking and brokerage world is in a growth phase that can last for years. Peter Lynch wrote that in the 1980s you just had to go to the mall to see investment opportunities in retailing stocks. In the '90s you have to open your eyes to the opportunities that exist right here on Wall Street.

Wall Street is sitting on a time bomb of the nicer sort, in that the public is moving its way. More investors are interested in stocks and bonds. Baby-boomers need to invest for their retirement. For 20 years money-market funds and real estate were the favorite investment outlets of the public. It took a decade to put $400 billion to $500 billion into money funds. Only in the 1990s has cash leaked from money funds into bonds and stocks, and the process will last at least another five years.

Your affection for financial stocks is a long-standing one, isn't it?

Yes, but we're heavier now than ever. We're in a financial sweet spot. There is overcapacity in the economy. Labor isn't asking for the moon. Competition will hold down interest rates and inflation to a degree. In this climate, the financial stocks can put together very good records.

The financial industry deals with a product called money, and money never becomes obsolete. In the 1980s banks really took risks with real estate, Third World loans and leveraged buyouts—all of which turned bad. They'll probably make new mistakes in a few years, but now the focus is on cleaning up risk and returning banks and thrifts and insurers to sound footing.

The government has done its part by issuing risk-based capital rules, which are forcing capital ratios higher. The good companies will gain market share from weaker sisters who can't expand because they're short of capital. They'll also gain market share by buying out competitors. So it seems there's opportunity for many financial companies to grow at an 8% to 15% rate. And many are selling for eight to 15 times earnings. The day may come when financial stocks are so popular that they're at a premium to the market multiple. Then we will have to look for other things. The pendulum swings, but I'm looking for long pendulum swings.

Let's say you didn't run this fund but were Joe Investor using the references at the public library. Would you still be as successful?

I think I would now, because I have a sort of data bank in my head—impressions and views on lots of companies and industries. One thing I focus on is the impression I have of management and its dedication to shareholder interest and its game plan for the future. One of my favorite questions is where they're putting the profits they generate, to enhance my return. What are they doing to build a moat around that business, to make it stronger?

So to answer your question, a thinking investor can operate anywhere. This means not chasing rainbows and fads and short-term results.

It's revealing of great money managers to know about their screwups. Student Loan Marketing—the stock that so excited Shelby Davis in 1993—didn't work out for Davis New York Venture. "I bought it as it slid from $48 to $40 a share, averaging $42," he said recently. "Then it went all the way to $34. At that point I decided I had been wrong. So as it started to rally, I sold it from $40 to $45. Now it is $66. That can happen. Pressure-point investing is not easy, because you're dealing with so many unknowns. At least a third of the time I make mistakes."

In 1993, Davis and his fund business were in a state of change. Son Chris was helping his dad, and in 1995 became Venture's co-manager as well as manager of the new Davis Financial fund. (Yet another Davis, older son Andrew, runs Davis Convertible Securities fund.) Plus, in 1993 Shelby Davis (later joined by Chris) took over management of Selected American Shares, a no-load growth-and-income fund. (New York Venture carries a 4.5% sales fee on its Class A shares and a deferred sales charge and higher expense ratio on its Class B shares.)

In speaking with Shelby and Chris again in 1996, I was struck by how much they think alike. In fact, there's a real continuum in the Davis family—Shelby's own father, Shelby Collum Davis, was a professional stock picker until age 80, and today the biggest shareholders of both Davis New York Venture and Selected American Shares are members of the Davis family. Says Chris: "When we have a bad day in the market, my dad says, 'You had better be proud of the stocks we own, because if this is the start of a bear market, we're going to own them a long time.' My dad also quotes my grandfather, who said you make most of your money during bear markets by what you buy—you just don't realize it at the time."

Chris describes the father-son team as "a 55-year-old brain with 30-year-old legs. There are companies that I follow most closely, and ones that Dad does. But there's not one stock in either Venture or Selected that we aren't both conversant about." Adds his father: "We love picking stocks and visiting companies. We have our own money—more than $100 million—in these funds. This is a family account, almost."

Davis New York Venture or Selected American—which is the fund to own? In theory, Selected is more income-oriented, the Davises say, and in fact it is a shade less volatile. But total returns of the funds in both 1994 and 1995 were almost indistinguishable, and you discover why when you examine their portfolios: 13 of the 15 largest holdings of Selected are also among the 15 largest holdings of Venture. Selected then did noticeably better in 1996 than Venture. So Selected is probably the better buy, if only because you save the 4.75% sales fee.

Foster Friess

Arefresher course on the relationship between hogs and portfolio management: Whenever Foster Friess adds a new stock to the portfolio of his Brandywine fund, he sells one (and sometimes two). The reason hearkens to his memory of hogs crowding around their feeding troughs on farms near Rice Lake, Wisconsin, where Friess grew up. When one hog bellied up to the trough, the weakest (or the least hungry) pig got shoved aside.

So it is with his portfolio, says Friess—the better ideas shove out the weaker investments. His associates heard this story one too many times and bought their boss a tiny piglet, since grown into a free-range hog. Now Friess is stuck with Wilbur, and you're stuck with his corny story.

Friess, born in 1940, has come a long way from Rice Lake. Today he divides his time among Greenville, Delaware (in the Brandywine Valley), Jackson, Wyoming, and Phoenix. And he has achieved what 99.9% of his fellow mutual fund managers have not: a superconsistent record of exceptional results. Each and every calendar year since Brandywine's beginning late in 1985, the fund has outperformed its peer group of long-term-growth funds, and across that span it did better than the overall stock market, too. During that decade, growth stocks had their day in the sun, and then undervalued stocks—not to mention big companies, then small, U.S. and international. All the while, Brandywine just kept producing those above-average returns. The only bad thing you can say about this fund is that it takes $25,000 to open an account.

KIPLINGER'S: How do you start the search for a stock to buy?

FRIESS: By reading the list of stocks that are hitting new highs.

That's certainly not a value investor's approach. What's the appeal of a stock hitting new highs?

What's the appeal of a stock hitting new lows?

Well, for one thing, it's cheap.

Yes, but why would anyone want to buy a company showing 5% earnings growth? Show me a stock that's selling for less than book value and I'll show you a dog.

Just what are you seeking when you scan that list of new highs?

Companies that will earn a lot more money. But we want that growth to be more than people expect. I want to buy a company whose earnings are growing 35% when everybody else thinks they're rising 25%.

You're looking for earnings growth of at least how much?

At least 25% annually.

How much are you willing to pay for that growth in terms of price-earnings ratios?

I don't like people saying, "This is a relatively cheap P/E ratio." I don't like relative comparisons because in 1962, when the multiples were 60 or 70 for the Nifty Fifty stocks, people said, "McDonald's is 60 times earnings and you can get Church's Fried Chicken for 38," and they got killed owning Church's when P/Es collapsed. So I start with an absolute number of 16.

What's magic about that?

I sort of picked it out. It's the kind of P/E ratio you'd expect from a Sara Lee or Eastman Kodak type of company.

If we attach a P/E of 16 to a steady blue-chip company, what should we pay for a company that's growing a lot faster? The answer is we don't like to pay more than 25 times earnings. For instance, if a company is growing at a 40% rate, I'm not going to pay

40 times its earnings to buy its shares.

The orientation toward lower P/E ratios is important in what we do. You take a lot of risk out of the equation if you pay 17 times earnings to buy a stock instead of 40 times earnings.

What sorts of questions do you ask about companies you become interested in?

We've developed a set of generic questions we can ask to learn, very quickly, if the company is worth pursuing as an investment. Why spend half an hour becoming highly knowledgeable about a company whose stock we're not going to buy? The questions themselves are proprietary, but I can tell you that they are always phrased as "What are analysts saying about your company?" and "What are you telling analysts about what they are saying?"

When we sense that a company is at odds with what Wall Street expects, that's a start-off point for our research. The companies we own are experiencing earnings growth of 56%, on average. Companies such as these change so quickly that Wall Street has a hard time keeping up with their dynamics. As a result, there is often inefficiency in the stock market because it takes longer for Wall Street to catch up with events. We can capitalize on that because our research process is streamlined. We can act quickly.

Your portfolio is overwhelmingly in medium-size and small companies. Do you care how big a company is?

No. What we do is independent of a company's size. It's not our intent to be a small-capitalization or even a mid-cap fund. It is our intention to find companies growing rapidly—faster than people expect—and to buy them at reasonable P/E ratios. An Eastman Kodak, a Du Pont or an Exxon is not going to fit that description. One-fifth of our assets are in companies with more than $3.5 billion in market capitalization. Another 35% is in companies with market caps of $1 billion to $3.5 billion, and the other 45% is under $1 billion.

You have a huge position in technology stocks—almost

half of the fund's assets. Is that intentional?

It isn't that I think technology is a great area and went out to buy things. Technology companies fit our criteria—rapid growth, reasonable P/Es, doing better than people expect. By definition, technology is a rapid-change area. So if a key ingredient to our fund's success is change, then technology stocks will be our raw material.

These companies do some highly specialized things. Do you insist on understanding their technologies before investing in them?

None of us here has an electrical engineering background. We're all generalists. The reason we've succeeded is because our research process gets us to call the customers of these companies and ask why they are buyers of these products. They'll tell us why—maybe because it's faster and cheaper. And we'll talk to a company's competitors, who are eager to tell you where the target company's weak underbelly is. They'll also acknowledge that a target company is a tough competitor or a price leader. They'll be candid.

With 268 stocks, one person would have a devil of a time keeping track of things. How do you divide the workload?

We're organized into five teams of three persons each. There isn't a lot of bureaucracy. There are no morning meetings. There's no vast committee that must approve each decision. It usually goes like this: A team comes up with an investment idea. The members call up the company's chief financial officer. They call suppliers. They call customers and competitors. If the company still looks good, they start buying. Very seldom will I say no.

Do all five teams use the same methodology? Or is there a growth team and a value team?

The challenge we have every day is to make sure we're following the style we've had for so long. It's not our style to bet on products that are not yet developing profits. If you come to me and say you found a great company that's going to lose money for two years but has a product coming along that's so powerful that by 1997 it will generate $2 per share in earnings, I'll say to come back to me when it starts making money.

Does this exclude investments in cellular-phone stocks, which have positive cash flow but no profits?

Absolutely. It also keeps us out of cable-TV stocks and biotechnology stocks. Nor will we own a Wal-Mart or Home Depot, which have great earnings growth but high P/E ratios. We would rather own a company with a lower multiple.

Getting back to Wilbur, your pet pig, how do you decide which stock to jettison when you introduce a new stock into your portfolio?

Each team has to leave in the computer a list of the $15 million worth of stock they would sell today if they had to sell. That's on the table as the least-favorite holdings—maybe three or four stocks per team. So when a new idea comes along, we go right to that list.

What would get a stock on that sell list? For instance, do you set target prices when you buy stocks?

Yes. When we buy a stock we ask what the earnings could be in, say, 18 to 24 months. And we also ask what potential P/E this stock can sell at. Let's say the answer is 22 times earnings. That gives us a potential price. We rank on a spreadsheet our potential appreciation in each stock, and when we need to sell something it's likely to come from the bottom of that list.

Over time, haven't you increased the number of stocks you hold in the fund?

Yes. That number gets adjusted as money comes in. Right now, we are getting $24 million a week in new money. The fund used to hold 250 stocks, but we've raised the number in recognition of our larger asset base. But the process of forced displacement continues.

How often do all your best efforts fail and you lose money on a stock?

Too often! To be exact, about 40% of the time. But in studies we've done, our top five or six winners wipe out all of the losses. The pigs-at-the-trough discipline lets us kick out things that aren't working.

What's your latest bitter disappointment?

DSC Communications—the old Digital Switch Corp. AT&T recently got some contracts that people thought DSC would get, and the stock dropped. I think that what I missed was that there were more expectations about that contract built into the stock price than I had thought. I had assumed that the stock price was being driven by earnings momentum. Sometimes what drives a stock is different from what I think, and if I don't pay attention I get my head handed to me.

Did you sell DSC Communications?

We're evaluating what to do. We originally bought it at only $8 and sold it at $59. Then we watched the stock for a while and bought it back at $53. Now it's $49 (the stock recently split).

Do you typically sell when you get taken by surprise like this?

No. It's a case-by-case thing. We always look forward. If your stock is down 25%, you don't walk around with your tail between your legs because you'll never win that way. Instead you say, "Okay, is it a buy at this price?" Look at the stock as if it had never gone down.

You've said Brandywine doesn't invest in markets but in companies. But in 1990 you abruptly went to 80% cash in the fund. Does that contradict your philosophy?

When something hits the system that nobody could have seen coming, that's different. The catalyst in 1990 was the invasion of

Kuwait, which occurred just as we were hit by a tax increase and budget cutbacks. With all that uncertainty, we sold a quarter-billion dollars in stocks in one day, and $800 million within a few days. [The fund still lost 25% in the brief bear market in 1990.]

Was this market timing?

You could call it that. You can't make a lot of money saying, "I think the Fed will do this, so I'll do thus-and-so." We don't do that. But this was a special circumstance.

Why the $25,000 minimum initial investment? Why not $1,000?

The fund was begun to accommodate our existing clients and the people who sat on the boards of our clients. We didn't want to go after the mass market. What happened was that we'd go, say, to Vanderbilt University to make a presentation on managing money, and somebody would come up to us in the hall and ask if they could invest $100,000 of their own money. It got to the point that we had 350 clients, and we needed to pool some of those assets.

Brandywine now has almost $2 billion in assets. When will you close the door to new investors?

We have a cutoff: $3 trillion. Seriously, the key to not having too many dollars to invest is to keep our culture lean and mean so that we don't develop a bureaucracy.

Within the next 18 months, going into 1996, Brandywine more than doubled its asset base, to $4.3 billion. By then, Friess Associates was managing a combined $8 billion in Brandywine, a sister fund and private accounts. The impact of this new money on Brandywine was predictable, in some respects. The fund narrowly trailed Standard & Poor's 500-stock index in both 1994 and 1995. The median market capitalization of its holdings almost tripled, to $3.4 billion, according to Morningstar Inc. Yet, ever true to his vow of mid 1994, Foster Friess sought to keep Brandywine nimble. One rule he instituted: Whenever his teams wanted to buy a new stock, they had to sell two. Thus, the number of holdings fell to 191. And the fund stocked up on fast-growing technology issues, to the point that its fortunes rose and fell with that sector in 1995.

His emphasis on focus may have had something to do with 1996's results, in which Brandywine ran ahead of the S&P 500 going into the final weeks. This is notable because very few funds in 1996—especially those with billions in assets—could say as much.

But the most exciting thing going on, in Foster's opinion, was the success his firm was having in harnessing technology. Friess Associates was conducting more and more of its business by e-mail and fax. This included contacts with a lot of chief financial officers of companies the fund invested in, and even extended to interaction within the firm. "All of our internal communication is done by e-mail and faxes, and we are discouraging all voice contact, because we think facts and opinions can be exchanged more easily in a written format. The written comments can be more thorough and in-depth."

Just how long the quiet extends was revealed in this anecdote: "Debbie Shippee, my right arm, and I decided to see one day how far we could take this concept of not talking to each other, and see how much we could get done." The experiment had its rough moments. Shippee handed Friess a note that said, "I can't read your handwriting." But at the end of the day, they added up the e-mails in and out, faxes in and out, plus phone calls to Friess that Shippee had intercepted and converted to e-mails and his written replies that she had relayed back to those callers. "They totaled 177," he reported. "Had I tried to do all this by telephone, I could have done 20 to 25, max."

He had even conducted an interview with a *Boston Globe* reporter via the Internet, and invited me to try it sometime. With some reluctance, I did. An excerpt from our electronic exchange:

KIPLINGER'S: The voiceless office: I am fascinated. . . . Is it based on a theory about productivity?

FRIESS: Absolutely an issue of productivity!

Or personal dislike of pointless meetings and idle chitchat?

It's not that I *dislike* meeting and chitchat; there are some nice warm feelings that flow from those activities but meetings should *not* be used to transfer information or make decisions. It is simply *highly* more productive to do it the way we do it. Friess Associates does not exist to meet the warm fuzzy needs of its members; it exists to make money for those who are counting on us.

As I recall, people at Friess Associates' meetings have no chairs—to keep such gatherings short. Still true? Are there still meetings?

Yup. The meetings we have are usually to recognize people or when people chemistry is important. But you are right. They are held in my office, where there are few chairs, so practically everyone stands. When managements or clients visit we do let them sit down!

Don't you fear looking like an idiot being quoted as saying you want to avoid voice contact among professionals at Friess Associates? Shades of Dr. Strangelove! Won't your shareholders think you are about to go to the funny farm? Join Wilbur?

Much of our success, I think, comes from wanting to do what is best and most productive for shareholders. Worrying about how we are perceived can get in the way, but obviously we prefer to be perceived as a *very* hard-hitting team that has effectively harnessed state-of-the-art technology that makes us look anything but like idiots, but instead as savvy barracuda types, who go to every length to win that which is within prudent risk parameters and appropriate ethical constraints.

Did you repeat the voiceless workday with Debbie?

Almost every day! Debbie and I communicate almost 100% by fax and e-mail unless there is a *time* element that requires voice. The other exception is when I may be out cross-country skiing or on the ski lift and I get an idea. I then call it in to a dictation machine and the transcriber then types it into e-mail for Debbie. I am conscious of saving her time as well.

No, Friess Associates isn't being run by a nut, I concluded. The working methods that he and his people follow are . . . ah, unusual. But who among us likes to be ruled by the tyranny of meetings and ringing telephones? Given the time and quiet to reflect on our investment decisions, maybe we'd all make better ones.

Rod Linafelter

I
f investing were a science, reducible to a few simple rules, we'd all be rich. But it's not, and nobody knows that better than Rod Linafelter. Born is 1959, this handsome young man once seemed to have the Midas touch. As the protégé of William Berger, he almost doubled investors' money in 1991 at Berger One Hundred fund. Linafelter produced market-beating returns in 1992 and 1993, too. Then he hit the wall. In 1994 One Hundred under-performed the overall stock market by eight percentage points, and in 1995, by 16 points. And 1996 wasn't so hot, either—by the end of November, One Hundred's total return of 15% paled beside the 25% gain of the Standard & Poor's 500-stock index.

Was Linafelter just lucky to begin with? Or did he have the sort of dry spell every disciplined money manager must expect from time to time? Given what had happened, a visit to Denver in 1996 to talk with Linafelter seemed in order.

KIPLINGER'S: How structured is your approach to picking stocks?

LINAFELTER: Pretty structured, because I'm always looking for the same thing: predictable earnings growth. Companies that have this can command premium prices. The art to this approach is to look forward and determine who has a business plan that can work and, if it can, how profitable it will be.

How much earnings growth do you demand—15% a year?
Everyone wants to pin me down to an absolute figure. It's all relative. In 1995, 20% earnings growth was not enough because you could get that from companies in the S&P 500.

And what exactly do you mean by predictable?
Companies that can meet or beat expectations quarter after

quarter. What really helps is to find more upside potential than the consensus expects.

So you don't just want a fast-growing stock with predictable earnings. You also want to believe it will do better than everyone thinks it will?

We're sensitive to value. You want to buy at the right price. I call this buying growth at a discount.

Your biggest holding today is WorldCom. How does it fit your stock-picking criteria?

It's the fourth-largest long-distance carrier. Earnings are increasing at a 20%-to-25% rate, and I look for them to continue to do that. Revenue isn't highly dependent on what is going on in the economy. We've owned the stock a long time.

Was WorldCom's price-earnings ratio sky-high when you bought it?

No. In fact, the P/E was lower than the rate of earnings growth. It is pretty hard to say an opportunity is undiscovered if a company is trading at a P/E multiple greater than its rate of earnings growth. I'll seldom buy a stock whose P/E ratio exceeds its growth rate.

Do you insist on meeting the people who run companies you invest in?

It's pretty rare that I haven't.

A lot of fund managers say the same thing. But don't you risk being sweet-talked by executives who have the gift of gab? Isn't the real proof of good management in the financial results?

That's true. A lot of successful companies have mediocre managers, and a lot of great managers run mediocre companies. But if I have a question, I don't want to go through a Wall Street analyst to get everything secondhand. I want to pick up the phone and call the appropriate manager.

Generally, how many stocks measure up to your criteria—a few or a lot?

I'm rarely short of ideas.

Then how do you decide which of many attractive stocks to buy?

I want to own companies other people will be attracted to at a later date and at a higher price. So I prefer stocks that have a good story attached to them.

And "a good story" means . . .

Something with a little sex appeal. Intel is a household name. But Intel can be an investment, as opposed to just a trade. That's because it controls not only its own destiny, through its computer microprocessors, but everyone else's destiny as well. Think of Intel this way: When its heart beats, blood flows throughout the technology sector.

But isn't Intel a very cyclical stock—closely tied to the economy?

If you look back over the years, you'll find that it really isn't all that cyclical. Personal-computer demand has been driven not only by demand from households but also from corporations. As long as the guys at Intel continue to drive the technology standards higher—and as long as you continue getting more power for less money—the company won't rise and fall with the economy. Everybody is seeking productivity enhancement, and your best tool is to use more technology. That's where Intel comes in.

Aren't earnings a bit erratic and unpredictable?

They are not as predictable as I would like. But at some point in time Intel will deserve a price-earnings ratio in line with the overall market's P/E. Right now it looks incredibly cheap. I think it can increase its earnings consistently at an annual rate in the mid-to-high teens. And as of early June, Intel was trading at about 16 times what we expect it to earn this year and 14 times the expected earnings in 1997.

Do you also seek out broad investment themes?

Yes, sometimes by happenstance. Oil-service stocks are an example. We started a year ago buying shares of Petroleum Geo-Services, which does three-dimensional seismic work. In researching this stock it became apparent we were at the threshold of a new oil-services cycle. I've always liked industries that have had a huge amount of capacity taken out. The survivors are truly the best companies. When we started researching one oil-service company, we realized that several were doing exceedingly well.

Nobody had heard a peep out of these companies for a decade.

You're right. They've been in a ten-year bear market. I still don't think people understand how much upside leverage these folks can get from additional revenues, as is starting to happen. In 1996 I'm expecting these companies, as a group, to increase earnings 45%, and next year another 30%. For a growth-fund manager, it's like finding a diamond in the rough. Oil services are now 16% of fund assets.

Have your stock-picking methods remained the same over the years?

Pretty much. I can say with a high degree of certainty that over time the share price will follow a company's ability to make money. There may be bumps in the road, but if earnings keep rising, so will the stock price.

That all sounds easy, but something didn't work as it should have in 1994 and 1995. Did you do anything differently?

No, we didn't. Berger One Hundred performed in line with other growth funds in 1994 until the devaluation of the Mexican peso, on December 21. About 7% of the fund's assets were in Mexico. We sold every stock that had dollar-denominated debt at once because the cost of borrowing money had just doubled for those companies.

I kept the other Mexican stocks for another week to try to assess the economic impact of the situation. Nobody had a clue. That cost us 3.5 percentage points of total return in 1994 and almost as much in 1995.

I remember standing in the shower on the first market day of 1995 and thinking to myself, "Okay, 1994 is behind us. Let's just start with a good, solid, up day, put the total return in the black, and never look back." I think we were down 2% on the first trading day of 1995. It was an ugly start to the year, and we had to dig out from that.

What else hurt you last year?

We'd been big owners of long-term-care companies—the nursing homes—for a long time. Then in early 1995 the Health Care Financing Administration made some proposals on reimbursement rates and that group took a hit. We hung on to those stocks too long, and it was certainly my error. I wanted to analyze the situation first, and it was unanalyzable. That cost us another three percentage points of total return.

As 1995 wore on, didn't you beef up technology stocks?

I didn't have to. We were already in the right names, and as they went up in price, technology became 35% of the portfolio. It was really difficult for me, because I'm a big believer in technology, but I said we couldn't allow this sector to keep getting bigger. One of my jobs is to manage the risk-reward equation, and you have to ask yourself who will buy those stocks at a higher price if everyone already owns them. Technology stocks dropped as low as 16% of assets but are back to 24% now.

So you lightened up on technology stocks in '95. Do you wish you'd ridden that horse longer?

In hindsight, certainly. I'm a very competitive person.

Do you ever wish you could just put on blinders and go with the flow?

What happens then is that I begin to stretch to make companies fit my criteria. You're accepting less from a growth standpoint, you're accepting less from the whole evaluation. You've got to be able to sit there and say that the potential gains outweigh the risks of making the investment. Otherwise, a Treasury bill would be the place to invest your money.

What have you learned from these experiences? Humility, perhaps?

Yes, although every time during the past five or six years that something good was written about me, I would take a few moments to shut the door and tell myself there would come a day when things wouldn't go well. Certainly they didn't go well last year.

Also, I have the best staff of analysts you could want. But it was difficult for me to become as comfortable with their recommendations as I would have been had I done all the research myself. I'd play the devil's advocate and wind up convincing myself more than anybody.

Did this cause you to miss some opportunities?

Yes, as much as anything through timing—being slow to make the right decisions.

How do you want to be judged at Berger One Hundred?

I'd love to be looked back on as someone who generated well-above-average long-term rates of return, and did it by being an investor, as opposed to a trader. I'm disappointed about 1995 but not discouraged. That wasn't the first time our investment philosophy underperformed, nor the last. But there will be plenty of years when we will be right at the front of the pack again.

The next year or two should speak volumes about Rod Linafelter's abilities running a growth-stock fund. One hallmark of a good money manager is consistency, and Linafelter stuck to his methods when good results weren't forthcoming.

Another hallmark is good-to-excellent investment returns. Berger One Hundred's total return in 1996 again trailed other long-term-growth funds and the stock market in general. Berger One Hundred's 225,000 shareholders must surely yearn for a reprise of the good old days—a bell-ringing year or two—and for Linafelter, the weight of those expectations is probably palpable.

Gary Pilgrim

Forget Peter Lynch. Gary Pilgrim is the best stock picker of the past five years and the past ten. As of late in 1996, no other diversified fund has done better during those time spans than PBHG Growth fund, which he founded in December 1985. The fund outperformed Standard & Poor's 500-stock index by 12 to 36 percentage points in four of the past five calendar years and was well-positioned to beat it again in 1996.

But unlike Lynch, Pilgrim, born in 1940, doesn't get his investment ideas at the shopping mall. He doesn't invest in what he knows best. In fact, the details of what a company does aren't of much interest to him. Nor does he care much what a company's management has to say. Price-earnings ratios? Ha! Price-to-book-value ratios? Don't even ask.

So how does Gary Pilgrim pick a stock? By finding reliable numbers that point him toward companies that are not just growing fast, but growing faster and faster. All this was explained one morning in mid 1996 across a conference table in the Philadelphia suburb of Wayne, Pennsylvania., which PBHG calls home. (PBHG, by the way, is the name formed by Pilgrim's initials and those of co-founder Harold Baxter, who handles marketing.)

KIPLINGER'S: Is your stock-picking system proprietary—a trade secret?

PILGRIM: No. Anyone could replicate it fairly easily, at least in concept. What makes it effective for me is that it really expresses things I feel strongly about and believe in as elements of making investment decisions. It's not somebody else's model that you refer to when you're in the mood. It's the backdrop against which we select every stock.

So explain how it works—how a stock finds its way into PBHG Growth.

First, it has to get in our sights. We have assembled a universe of 1,000 or so stocks. No good growth company should escape our net—we want to watch all of them. So if a company has increased its earnings 20% or more for a couple of quarters, if it looks like a pretty good company, if it's not terribly erratic, if it has at least the appearance of sustainable growth—then it goes into our universe.

And then you invest in it?

Oh, no. Then my ranking system takes over. It ranks all 1,000 stocks, and from among the top 30%, the portfolio managers of all PBHG funds are expected to select stocks to buy initially.

Think of the ranking as a great big productivity tool. The ranking captures all the elements we think are important to our type of investing. You can talk about a stock until you're blue in the face. You can listen to everyone's expectations for it. You can hear brokers blow smoke up your ears about what a great company it is. But if it doesn't have the criteria to rank it high on our list, then you put it on the back burner and buy something else.

What are the criteria you use?

Above all, I'm looking for upward revisions in the earnings estimates that analysts make. This accounts for 35% of the ranking score, and it simply compares the estimates today with a prior period.

Is this a way to discover earnings momentum—company earnings that are rising at a faster and faster rate—before the companies actually report those earnings?

Exactly, and related to that is the next element, which accounts for 25% of the ranking score: earnings surprises. The more a company surpasses what smart analysts expect each quarter, the better.

Do you just average all of the estimates to determine when profits are higher than expected?

No. Not all analysts are created equal. In both earnings estimates and earnings surprises, I want numbers from the most credible analysts. We know each of these people and have an opinion about who's good on a certain stock, who's flaky or erratic, who's slow to notice things and who's fast.

The two earnings elements have to do with expectations. The other 40% of the ranking system involves actual and expected growth in sales and earnings. For instance, we compare actual year-over-year growth in both sales and profits each quarter to see if it is accelerating. In other words, it's not enough for me to know a company is growing at a 20% rate. If that 20% is down from 40%, I want the system to reflect that the rate of growth has been slowing. So our system figures the rate of acceleration or deceleration.

Another measure we use, although it is probably the least important part of the computer model, is to calculate in a variety of ways what we believe to be the underlying, long-term growth rate of the company. There are about ten ways we come up with that number, and they are statistical measures rather than our own guesses.

You don't stick a wet finger in the wind and say, "Well, looks like a 20% grower?"

None of that, because that's what we see other people doing, and I don't like to constantly change our growth rates based on whatever piece of paper I picked up this morning, or who I spoke to last.

Does your system often overestimate the long-term rate of earnings growth?

I don't think it does. The financial world chronically under-estimates how long a company can sustain a high rate of growth, and our model tends to calculate expected growth rates that are higher than the consensus. That's because we look only at what is actually transpiring. We don't guess when the rate is going to slow or by how much. Most analysts think that if a company is growing at a 50% annual rate today, nine months from now that rate will slow to 30%. I don't see any value in that.

And speaking of value, why don't you crank into your

equation any measure of value? You've said nothing about wanting low price-earnings ratios, low price-to-book-value ratios or nice yields.

Valuation has no role in a growth portfolio. It is a waste of my time to wonder if companies I like are overvalued or undervalued.

Doesn't it defy common sense to buy stocks with sky-high P/E ratios?

Does it defy common sense to buy companies whose earnings are increasing 80% per year? See, that's the problem: Everybody holds those P/E ratios out there as if they mean something by themselves. A P/E of 40 doesn't mean anything unless you look at the underlying growth characteristics of the stock. You'll find that the high-P/E stocks are all selling at numbers commensurate with their growth rates.

Are you saying that people who like to buy growth stocks when they have reasonable P/E ratios—growth-at-a-price investors—are all wet?

No. There are a lot of ways to skin a cat. I'm just trying to perfect the way I do it.

What about "price momentum"? Do you want the stock price to be rising when you buy a stock?

No. I put about the same weight on price momentum as I do on P/E ratios. There's so much "noise" in what causes stocks to go up and down—I don't say this glibly. We have tried to build valuation models such as P/E ratios and price-momentum models into our system, but when we do, it doesn't raise the level of our returns.

Do you back up your statistical research by getting to know the managements of these companies?

I don't see any value in knowing them. Speaking for myself, personal impressions of people get in the way of evaluating a possible investment. I don't like to find myself thinking, "Oh, I like this guy," or "He seems a little sleazy; I don't trust him." Such impressions are not reliable. And companies don't come around to tell you a bad story. So I've decided not to have opinions about managements.

Wouldn't it help to know what they think is happening to their company?

It would, occasionally. Some of my associates who run our other funds do talk to these companies, and they tell me what they learn. That's a better use of my time than going to meeting after meeting. Let me put it another way: I could spend the rest of my life trying to understand the technical side of Ascend Communications, my biggest holding, but it wouldn't help me as a portfolio manager. My objective is to know how these companies are doing as opposed to what they are doing. It's much more important to know that analysts are raising earnings estimates, that competitors aren't gaining ground, that controversies over products are being resolved. In other words, I want my knowledge to be a mile wide and an inch deep.

How often do you take these statistics and run them through the meat grinder to get a ranking?

Once a week. Then we assign a decile rank to each stock. A perfect score is a 10.

Are there any perfect companies among the 1,000 in your universe?

Four of them. Radisys is one. It's some sort of software company.

Do you own it?

No. It's too small for PBHG Growth. Then there's Scopus Technology, which is also too small. I do own APAC TeleServices and HFS, the other two "10" stocks.

Do you start at the top of the list and buy the highest-ranked stocks?

Not exactly. If five stocks are rated 10 and I don't own three of them, I'll review those I don't own to make sure I have good reasons not to. The ranking system puts everything in place at a certain time. But the ongoing mission for every one of us is to anticipate change. That's the art. If I get a call from an analyst who tells me he's raising his estimate for APAC TeleServices, and the stock is rated 8 instead of 10, I know that when we get that fact in our system and run the ranking again, APAC is going to score higher. That's exactly what I want to see in a stock, and I won't wait for it to be reranked before I buy it. The system allows us to be very well organized about a large number of companies.

Do you sell a stock when it slips down in the ranking?

That's exactly right. My highest-ranked stocks I'm always adding to. When a stock drifts down, it gets less emphasis and is gradually sold from the portfolio. Again, it's because stocks at the top of the ranking consistently produce better returns than those in the middle.

PBHG Growth has had some incredible years. But now the fund's assets are at $5 billion. Can you keep beating the market year after year?

We have yet to prove we can manage large amounts of money as well as we managed small amounts. But so far, so good. The size of the company I invest in doesn't really explain our results. It has more to do with the fact that we've been in a growth-stock market since 1991 and that we have an above-average method of finding good growth stocks. When the tide runs out—when growth-stock investing goes into one of its periods of underperformance—then you can ask whether I've lost my touch.

What would you do in a big down market? Sell stocks and go to cash?

I can't predict how high a stock will go, or how low, and the last thing I want to do is turn loose a perfectly good company that is doing everything it is supposed to do, just because its price is falling. See, the problem with getting in and getting out is that if you don't know what something is supposed to be worth, why get in or out? And when do you get out? When it is down 5%? Ten percent? Thirty percent? Who knows! And it can reverse in an instant. When companies begin to deteriorate fundamentally, I sell them. But I won't sell them just because they're volatile.

PBHG keeps bringing out new funds: Emerging Growth, Core Growth, Select Equity, Large Cap and Limited. Except for the size of the typical company they invest in, they seem indistinguishable. How do you tell them apart?

You said it: By the market capitalization of their portfolios. I don't want someone to stay away from PBHG because they think all we do is small-company growth investing. But all these funds you named invest from the same ranking of stocks that I use at PBHG Growth, so it shouldn't surprise anyone that the characteristics of these portfolios are so similar, or that their total returns should often be so close.

What would cause you to close PBHG Growth to new investors?

If the fund grew so large that we owned more of a company's shares than I felt comfortable owning. The only alternative would be to own more stocks or to own bigger companies. So far, we've opted to let the bigger companies creep into the portfolio while holding the line on the number of stocks. This may be a good solution.

When a fund has proved itself the very best over a very long time, you have to wonder what its manager did that others did not. Sometimes it's hard to isolate the reasons. But Gary Pilgrim's investing methods are clearly defined, and certain qualities stand out:

- **He avoids emotion.** His reliance on what is knowable—the facts he cranks into his ranking system, all having to do with earnings growth—over opinion and guesswork is a powerful plus if he seeks the right facts.

- **He knows what's important.** His rankings give over-whelming weight to two events: upward revisions in earnings estimates (a predictor that a stock will have an increasing rate of profit growth) and greater-than-expected quarterly earnings (confirmation of that prediction). As a result, PBHG Growth will own this kind of stock early rather than late.

- **He knows what's not important.** He wears blinders when it comes to P/E ratios and other yardsticks of value. This is heresy to all investors in undervalued stocks and to many growth-stock investors as well. But "cheap" and "overpriced" are terms that don't apply to the sort of investing he does. Nor does he care to listen to CEOs of companies he invests in; what they have to say hasn't proved useful to him in the past.

James Stowers III

The way Twentieth Century funds invest is simply outrageous. Would you buy a stock with a price-earnings ratio of 100? Twentieth Century funds will. Moreover, its people may not even notice what the P/E of a particular stock is. They simply don't care.

Twentieth Century's growth funds use an aggressive, almost dare-you investment approach devised in 1971 by James Stowers Jr., the founder of this Kansas City-based company. His system looks for stocks with accelerating earnings and a rising price—and the devil with almost everything else. Under the right circumstance, such as a strong upward stock market, this system yields incredible total returns. Twentieth Century Ultra returned 86% in 1991, and sister fund Vista, 74%. Let the market go the other way and this system delivers breathtaking losses—in a three-month period of 1990, Ultra plummeted 29% and Vista 40%, versus the S&P 500's 19% fall. The secret, of course, is that over time the stock market goes up more than down. And over time, most Twentieth Century funds have done wonderfully.

James Stowers Jr., now in his seventies, is today the gray eminence of Twentieth Century funds. His day-to-day role has been assumed by son James Stowers III, born in 1959, who also serves as lead manager of two of Twentieth Century's best-known funds, Growth and Ultra.

Among the challenges facing the younger Stowers is demonstrating that his father's pedal-to-the-metal techniques remain valid. Twentieth Century growth funds performed unevenly during the first half of the 1990s, giving rise to doubts about their investment strategies. When I initially spoke with Stowers III in Kansas City in the autumn of 1994, responding to those doubts was very much on his mind.

KIPLINGER'S: When you pick stocks, are you concerned with anything but the rate of increase in earnings?

STOWERS: It's acceleration in the rate of earnings growth that we seek—not just high earnings growth. A 5% rate of growth may excite us more than a 50% rate if that 5% compares with the previous quarter that may have been growing at 1%, and the quarter before that may have been down 20%.

You focus on actual rather than estimated earnings. Doesn't this tend to get you into a stock at a higher price, and thereby increase your risk?

If the growth rate is high enough and the outlook is positive enough, we can make up for this. We purchased Amgen and U.S. Surgical after the stocks had already doubled. But if they look as if they will go up sixfold or eightfold, we're not as concerned about the first 10%—or even the first 50%—of the move.

Do you care about sales growth?

Yes, because if there's a cost-cutting program, it will have a limited life. In most cases, when you start cutting costs by cutting jobs or closing plants, you eventually run that out and you've got to look at the top line—sales—to see if the enterprise is actually growing.

Could you describe how this stock-picking process works?

It starts when the company reports its quarterly results. That would be when we see acceleration in earnings. Our computer will flag the stock and define its acceleration in one of 32 different ways.

Why 32 ways?

There's pure acceleration in profits, but numbers aren't always perfectly lined up—when earnings grow 30% this quarter, 20% last quarter and 5% the quarter before that. An acceleration code of 1 is when earnings and sales are up for one quarter. A code 2 is when both are accelerating for two quarters, and 3 is three consecutive quarters of acceleration. Typically a 3 with big numbers is best. I should add that we adjust for extraordinary events, and we like to go back two to four years—to a record year—to see whether a company is breaking out of a trend line that it has been growing in. If you get above that trend line, it's a pretty significant change.

All this is interpreted for you by your computer?
Most of the time. It doesn't work as well on a lot of industries, such as insurance and banking. For them we define acceleration in different ways—such as acceleration of current assets, or acceleration in the improvement of their portfolios.

Let's say a stock you don't own shows up as a code 3 on the computer. What happens then?
Hopefully we'll be on top of it immediately. If the numbers look reasonable, we'll consider buying the stock that day.

No committee to make decisions?
No. We do want to make sure those numbers are clean—not an apples-versus-oranges thing—that the "story" behind the acceleration is intact and that this isn't a one-quarter phenomenon. And we want to get a feel from the company that acceleration is likely to continue.

What you have not been describing is fundamental research—who runs the company, how well they do it, estimates of what the profits will be this year and next, projected earnings-growth rates into the next century and all that stuff. That isn't your game, is it?
No. We don't have to do that. The companies we buy are growing so fast that if they have an ugly balance sheet, their growth rates are such that they generate cash to fund that balance sheet. So it's just not a concern.

So valuation—a stock's price-earnings ratio, for example— plays no part in your decisions?
Very little. John Neff [a value-oriented investor—whose interview

for this book begins on page 30—who ran Vanguard Windsor fund until his retirement at the end of 1995] would not last a week here. His style works. But our style works, too. I'd have a hard time buying one of his stocks and having to wait so long. His stocks certainly have less volatility. But I feel as good owning some of our stocks because I think our pot at the end of the rainbow may be bigger than his.

We've been discussing earnings momentum. But don't you also practice price momentum—waiting until the stock price is visibly rising?

Yes. If the world doesn't see what we see, then the stock may not go anywhere for a long time. You really want to see some improvement in the investment world's opinion of a stock, and it shows up in the price.

Part of the reason our style works is that we assume management has no idea how big things are getting in their own organizations. And Wall Street has no idea what P/E ratio to put on rapidly growing companies. So when volume runs up and a stock starts to take off, we will be in it. If someone wants to criticize us for being too enamored of some numbers and charts, and the stock ends up tapering off, did we run it to an extreme price? Sure. But we weren't alone.

Somebody described this as bandwagon investing. But my feeling is why wait for two years for the stock to move, when you can put your money on another stock that is already moving higher. I'd rather be where the action is.

Doesn't buying after the price has already risen add to the risk of your funds?

Here's how I look at the risk: The analysts may say that earnings will turn up, but if we were to go into a stock just based on the enthusiasm of Wall Street and some optimistic expectations, and an earnings disappointment occurred, we're really hurt. So we'll give up the first 10% or 20% or 30% move in a stock in exchange for knowing that earnings and revenues are accelerating and the stock price is rising.

By that same token, you don't pay attention to P/E ratios when deciding when to sell?

No. The stocks we buy have growth rates such that Wall Street has no idea what they're worth. These stocks tend to move to extreme valuations. We bought MCI Communications at 100 times trailing earnings and made six to eight times our money.

But it's fair to say that being value-insensitive adds to the volatility of your funds.

Very much.

Is the decision on selling the reverse of that on buying—sell when the acceleration of earnings begins to decelerate?

Pretty much. It's not always black and white. A company can report a slowdown but maybe there's something happening behind the scenes, such as a missed contract or maybe they're three months away from a big new product. We may decide to put a yellow flag on the stock instead of selling it. So a call to the company and a little more homework on data other than earnings may keep us in a stock longer.

Does the fact that more people are trying to be acceleration investors make it harder for you to succeed?

What helps us is that people can't stick to the discipline that this system requires. If they did, it would be harder for us.

Where do others fall off the wagon?

Valuation. They love the idea of earnings acceleration. They love growth stocks. They love all the technical aspects. But they get dizzy real easy. They get too uncomfortable owning stocks with sky-high P/Es.

Do you apply the same investment techniques to Twentieth Century International Equity?

We regard these methods as we do gravity, and gravity works in all parts of the world. There are more undiscovered stocks overseas, so there has been more emphasis on value. If we can get high growth and the valuations are low, too, then we will take advantage of that.

Your funds do poorly in narrow markets like we had in 1994. They do terribly in a strong downward market. When will they do best?

In a straight-up market. We've been a lot more concerned lately about the losses that can occur in these funds in down markets. When we get into a bear-market trend, we do not second-guess our numbers and we don't have a lot of tolerance for slowing acceleration—we're out quickly and into something else.

Are you disappointed with the results of your major growth funds in 1994?

It has not been our market. It has been tough. You look at a chart of the Dow or the S&P 500 and it just kind of waffles.

But results vary a lot between similar funds. For example, Twentieth Century Vista has been gasping for breath. In four out of five years since 1989, Ultra outperformed Vista in terms of returns, despite the similarity of the stocks they prefer. What is going on?

Vista was hurt the worst in 1990, when it was down 16% and Ultra was up 9%. Back in 1990, the P/E ratios of the biotech and computer and health care stocks were very high. Vista's lead manager—he's no longer here—moved the fund out of the higher-P/E stocks late in 1990. And in the strong upward market that followed in 1991, high-P/E stocks outperformed low-P/E stocks.

Are you saying that the mistake was to let Vista invest too conservatively?

Yes. Allowing Vista to own stocks outside its valuation parameters was a mistake on our part. If the managers of one of our funds do not live up to the charter of the fund, then it's our fault for poor management, and that's why you see my name on Vista sometimes. I have to drive the management of that fund, even though I'm not in there day to day to sit at their meetings. But they know I'm looking over their shoulders.

There are some pretty heavy-duty mandates on us in terms of Vista's performance. The numbers have been much better for Vista lately. Back when it was not performing well, the average earnings-growth rate for its portfolio was lower than for the stocks Ultra owned, and Vista's average P/E ratio was higher. So it was paying more for less growth. Now the average earnings-growth rate of Vista is 41%, and Ultra's is 27%.

So what, specifically, are you telling the people who run Vista?

The new managers very quickly learned that you can't mess around with new, fresh acceleration by a small-cap stock. When these things report their earnings, you can't sit on them and let them get stale. You look at the numbers, you confirm what you see and you buy it. If it fits, if the product makes sense, if the financial numbers are clean, if earnings are a good apples-to-apples comparison, you're better off buying now because the biggest moves occur in only 1% of the months. If you're not there, you're going to lose 95% of your return. And later, if you try to guess when these stocks have topped, you going to be shaken out way too early. That's what happened with the prior team.

If somebody were to ask you which of your funds to invest in, is Vista your best bet?

For somebody who has money looking to grow, and who can handle the volatility, Vista is clearly the fund to buy. Think about it: It is a smaller fund—$700 million in assets, versus Ultra's $10 billion— owning smaller companies than Ultra. It can move much more quickly. The growth rate of its average stock is much higher. It should perform better.

Then there is Twentieth Century Select. Its returns relative

to other funds owning large companies have slowed and slowed. Does your system not work well with large companies?

You obviously don't have the leverage with big-company names that you do with small companies. We're looking at Select right now. Every stock it owns must pay a dividend. So being restricted from owning a stock such as Microsoft, which pays no dividend, doesn't help. We do not want a fund restricted in such a way that it could hamper performance. If we could alter the dividend requirement to maybe 85% rather than 100% of the portfolio, that may allow enough freedom to rejuvenate the fund.

We're not sitting on the sidelines. This fund will perform better. We've got people whose compensation will be tied to this fund, starting with me and working down.

The size company that Ultra invests in has grown markedly since 1991, but it still seems full of juice. What keeps it alive and well?

Even though the stock-market value of its median holding has risen from $1 billion to $2.3 billion, we continue to try to buy small companies. In late 1992 Ultra owned 94 stocks. Today it has 150, and that number will be more than 200 soon. And Ultra is just over 30% in foreign stocks.

Traditionally, Twentieth Century has not said which people run which of its growth funds. Could you tell us?

Chris Boyd, Derek Felske and I, with the help of some senior analysts, take care of Ultra and Growth. Glenn Fogle, Jim Stark and their analysts run Vista and Giftrust. Chuck Duboc and Nancy Prial work on Select and Heritage.

I listened that morning to what Stowers said about Twentieth Century Vista, and upon concluding the interview took the elevator to the lobby, entered the fund company's customer-service center and on the spot transferred my account in Twentieth Century Growth fund, which I had nurtured for more than a dozen years, straight over to Vista. I hope that a lot of other people, upon reading that interview, did the same thing, because young Stowers was true to his word: Twentieth Century Vista *did* undergo a remarkable rejuvenation. Its turnaround was already evident when we spoke late in 1994, and the following year—one of those years made in heaven for Twentieth Century funds, because the stock market flew almost straight up, verging on mania at times—Vista was the place to be. Loaded to the gills with technology stocks, it sailed right past the S&P 500 index to return a lusty 46%, versus 38% for Giftrust and Ultra, 23% for Select and 20% for Growth.

My associate Manuel Schiffres was back in Kansas City during the latter weeks of 1995 to speak again with Stowers III. In the course of their conversation, Stowers made some perceptive comments about the growth funds stabled by Twentieth Century:

GIFTRUST. "Smallness matters. You can buy 10,000 shares of a small company and make it 3% of the fund, and then you can sell those shares in a flash and go on to something new. It's very nimble." But while the fund's managers can be nimble, investors in the fund cannot. You can invest money only in someone else's name and must agree not to let that person withdraw it for at least ten years. So this is not a fund for just anyone.

ULTRA. "Ultra will invest in stocks of all sizes—whatever it takes to create performance. Ultra is becoming a [Fidelity] Magellan. It's the kind of fund that if created today, you'd have a tough time selling to investors because when you tell people you're going to buy big companies and small companies, that you'll go overseas and maybe have 30% to 40% of assets in foreign companies, people can't pigeonhole it. The charter for Ultra, as with Magellan, is very broad. It's an all-cap fund."

VISTA. "I like the dicier opportunities. If we had a new small-cap fund, I'd put all my new money in there. So if I weren't here, I'd put all my money in Vista. Given what Glenn Fogle and his team have done, Vista should outperform Ultra. There are going be markets when bigger-company names outperform smaller-cap names. But the fact remains that Vista owns companies that are growing faster than what

Ultra can buy, because they are smaller companies. My job on that
fund right now is to review all their trades every week, to review all
their holdings by industry and by stock, and to provide feedback. The
feedback is very minimal, because I'm not seeing deviations from
what I'd be doing myself." Vista's asset size more than doubled in
1995, to $1.8 billion, and reached $2.5 billion by late 1996.

By then, however, Stowers must have been reviewing a lot of
Vista's trades once again. The fund laid a goose egg. It started the
year poorly in relation to other momentum-type funds, got the wind at
its back again by May, lost its gains entirely in the high-tech
massacre between late May and late July and scarcely recovered.
Giftrust, run by the same team, looked even worse. Both funds ended
November with low single-digit returns—this when the overall
market was up by 25%. This can be partially explained by the nature
of the stock market in 1996, when large companies did noticeably
better than small companies (the kind that Vista would invest in) and
undervalued small companies did better than fast-growing small
companies (again, Vista stocks). Still, the funds stank.

And the funds that had caused the most concern, Select and
Growth, got a new breath of life in 1996. Shed of its dictum that all its
holdings had to pay dividends—and helped by the fact that this was a
year benefiting large, growing companies—Select stayed neck-and-
neck with the S&P 500 throughout the year and turned in its best
performance.relative to other long-term growth funds since 1990.
Growth had almost as good a year.

Conclusion: Earnings-momentum investing works best with
small companies. And mutual funds with modest assets do better
than larger mutual funds. For most investors drawn by Twentieth
Century's aggressive ways, Vista remained the place to be. Given the
treacherous waters in momentum investing, only the bravest and
most committed individuals should try doing this on their own, and
the 1996 results for Vista and Giftrust showed that even the pros
have trouble walking the high wire sometimes.

Garrett Van Wagoner

D uring the late 1970s and early 1980s, when Peter Lynch had those sensational years at Fidelity Magellan—years so good that ever since people have looked for "the next Peter Lynch"—Magellan never ranked any higher than sixth among diversified U.S. funds during a calendar year. Of course, if you string together consecutive years of being sixth and ninth and 14th among hundreds of funds, pretty soon you'll have a cumulative record that nobody can touch . . . that is, until someone comes along and does the same thing, only better.

Enter Garrett Van Wagoner, born in 1955, and almost young enough to be Lynch's son. He has now run mutual funds exactly four years, and what a prodigy. Here are the total returns he generated and the standing of his fund each year among all diversified U.S. stock funds:

1993	58.5%	(1st)
1994	28.7	(1st)
1995	69.0	(3rd)
1996*	31.1	(3rd)

* to November 1

Those first three years were spent at Govett Smaller Companies. Then on the last day of 1995, he left Govett to begin his own fund group, bearing his name. The largest of his three funds, Van Wagoner Emerging Growth, achieved the 1996 results noted above.

If he keeps this up, we really will have a new living legend. And that poses the obvious questions: How in the devil did this guy compile such a record? And is it sustainable? Only time will tell whether Van Wagoner can stay at the front of the pack, and for how long.

But his highly individualized manner of investing sheds some light on how those huge returns were achieved. Unfortunately, his ways are not ones that most individual investors would find easy to duplicate. To learn what makes Garrett run, join our discussion one afternoon late in 1996, in Van Wagoner's three-room world head-quarters in downtown San Francisco.

KIPLINGER'S: In a nutshell, describe how you invest.

VAN WAGONER: I'm looking for companies with huge market opportunities, a leading product and a group of people surrounding it that is really excited about that opportunity.

That sounds easy. How do you actually do it? Where, for instance, do your ideas come from?

I try to stay wide open. Some ideas come from trade magazines. I read five or six a week in the technology and health care fields. I don't get much from brokerage analysts; they're in business to generate trading commissions, not to give me good ideas.

I do use Wall Street a lot, but the investment bankers rather than the traditional analysts.

You mean, people involved in initial public offerings of stock?

All emerging-growth managers look at IPOs. They're a great source of new ideas. I'll call the investment banker at XYZ and say, "Hey, do you know anything about the deal ABC is doing?" This person may know a lot about the company going public, even if his firm isn't involved. Often I will call around and ask why a firm is not involved in a particular IPO.

So you get a name of a company you never heard of. What next?

I'll do a preliminary look at the financials, just to see if it qualifies as the kind of company I want. That would mean a company whose earnings and revenues have been moving forward at all points in time and haven't been on roller-coaster rides. I want to see growth—at a minimum, 20% a year. And I'll look at the balance sheet, too, just to make sure there's not much debt. All of this I can get off an online databank, such as Compustat.

How much time has passed so far?

Five minutes. If the company fits my financial model, then I ask whether the industry is interesting to me and whether the company would be interesting. Depending upon the industry, I'll know a lot about it or a little. I'll start calling people to fill in my information blanks about the competitive forces within the industry and about the company itself—what's going on in that business, who are the winners and who are the losers, who's jockeying for position, where this company fits relative to its peers, whether it is considered a leader or in the second tier.

Who are you calling?

Anybody who can provide information. I might at this point call a brokerage analyst. If it were a life insurance company specializing in single-premium deferred annuities, I'd ask the insurance analyst who the top-quality players in that field are and what he knows about them, who has the best product, who historically has been a leader.

Do you have a sort of "kitchen cabinet" of consultants you call?

Yeah! Some are corporate executives who invest in my funds, in fact. But I've also got, say, in semiconductors, three or four people I've known for ten years who are active in that industry and will let me take five minutes of their time to ask what they know about a company. They might say, "Oh, I hear they're hiring like crazy, the product's selling great," or "Geez, I hear people are leaving; you don't want to go near them."

How many calls will you make about a company before you have a good fix on it?

Five to 15. I try to make it simple. If I get bogged down in developing an investment scenario around a stock, I get turned off pretty rapidly. You've probably heard the saying that if you can't write the essence of an idea on the back of a matchbook, it probably isn't a good idea. Well, if I can't understand very quickly why a product is so broadly needed, I lose interest.

Now you've spent an hour on this stock. . . .

And I have a basic idea of what the world thinks of this company's position within its industry and a basic idea of the corporate history. Maybe I know a little bit about senior management. At this point I'll probably call the company directly.

And ask for the investor relations department?

Never. Investor-relations people are hired to tell you nothing. I'll ask for either the chief executive or the chief operating officer. Most of the time it's the same person in a small company.

How often will this person take your call?

Half to two-thirds of the time. Some CEOs could care less about Wall Street; if they could take their companies private again, they would.

But if you get the boss on the phone, what will you ask?

I don't take the high-handed approach. I explain that I've heard some very interesting things about the company, that I'm doing some followup work and would like to spend a few minutes to ask some basic questions. Hopefully, this will lead to half an hour's conversation. With most companies I want to know two basic things: where it and its products are positioned within the industry, and how it intends to sell its product—in other words, its methods of distribution, whether by direct sales force, through agents or through distributors.

Why is the method of distribution so important?

Because I've seen lots of companies with great products that get distribution all screwed up and just fizzle out. Some products should be sold through a direct sales force, and some not. IBM invented the personal computer, so why didn't it become the number-one PC vendor? Because it had college-educated white males with large expense accounts selling million-dollar mainframe computers who couldn't be bothered selling a $15,000 PC system.

If you never get that first phone call returned by the boss, will you invest in the company anyway?
He'd have to throw away a few messages from me before I stop trying. But the stock would have to be incredibly compelling for me to own it without talking to management.

Of the stocks you look at, what proportion do you buy?
One out of ten—maybe one out of eight.

And if the idea survives past the point of calling the company, what proportion do you end up owning?
One out of three. What turns me off at that point would be the feeling that their plan won't succeed, or my suspicion that management doesn't have a plan—just a product.

You can tell just by talking to the chief executive?
Sure. You see that a lot in technology, where a mad scientist/inventor is the CEO. The problem is, they may have no idea how to run a business.

When you hang up the phone from talking to the CEO, is it still the day you first looked at this stock?
It could be.

Now you rush in and buy, right?
Oh no. Now I'll sit back and digest what I've learned, maybe come up with some additional questions. I may call competitors of this company and ask about the product, and take what competitors say and ask the company about its reaction.

All this presumes you know a lot about the industries in which you invest. Do you?
Yes. Two weeks ago I was at a big trade show in Atlanta that had

all the data communications companies. I spent three days walking between booths, looking at potential investments, current investments, competitors of these companies, and so on. It's important that if I'm going to put millions of dollars in a company I know what it does.

At the end of all this, what makes you decide whether to invest or not?

If I see a big opportunity for the company, if I think the management is motivated and can execute its business plan, and if I think the stock is appropriately priced, then I'm going to make money. If I'm right on my analysis over a reasonable length of time, say, 12 to 18 months, I can make money in such a stock under any market environment other than some kind of crash.

Can you illustrate these investment methods by taking us through the process that led you to add a stock to one of your funds' portfolios?

Sure. Adtran is based in Alabama. I've known about it for three years but never had a good understanding of its products. Adtran sells equipment to the telephone companies to allow increased throughput of data in the telephone network. You stick one of its devices on either end and it speeds things up. But they recently developed a rather unique product that has done well in the ISDN market, which is a protocol used on the Internet. This was one of the companies I was going to check out at the trade show in Atlanta.

I talked to a bunch of people at its booth—senior field people, not top management. Then I spoke with the chairman for about an hour. But the reason I got involved in the stock was because its price was declining, and I discovered that two funds were dumping its shares because they had changed managers and the new people didn't know Adtran, didn't like it, or whatever. So with the price coming down, I decided now was the opportune time to be a buyer.

So you really do care about whether a stock is overvalued . . .

I don't believe any price is a good price. I ask, "At this price, can I make money in this stock in the next 12 to 18 months in a flat market?" Another way to put it is, "What will people be paying for this stock a year from now?" I don't look at price-earnings ratios and say a P/E of 16 is a buy but 24 is too much. Different industries carry different P/Es, and a lot of it has to do with fashion on Wall Street. When I got into this business, if you had an energy-technology stock it would carry a P/E of 30 or 40 or 50. Now computer technology has been the rage for a while. Fashions change.

Which raises a question: What would happen to you, with your body of knowledge on computer and health care technology, if these fields became passé?

I'd learn new businesses. The way my process works is this: If all of a sudden a bunch of companies start doing better and are in the small-cap arena, I'll probably hear about it. I'll be curious. Lately it has been energy services. I hadn't invested in those companies in years. I heard some chatter that things were getting better last summer. So I started doing some work and discovered things really were starting to turn. I found one idea—one stock—to explore, then two and then four. Next thing I knew I had ten or 12 of them.

If retailing gets hot, I'm going to hear about one retailer, then I'll hear about two, three, four, and my focus will turn. This is one of the reason my funds do so well. I don't sit down and say I'm going to be in technology or health care. I own these companies because they're doing really well. It's all from the bottom up.

What do you think made you so spectacularly successful at Govett, and so far in '96 at your own funds?

I'm not sure I know. I'm flexible to the ideas I get. I have a very fast trigger—if I don't like what I hear, I have no patience with a stock. I won't wait for trouble to show up in the numbers. I want to anticipate the trouble.

Didn't much of your big returns come from initial public offerings?

At Govett in 1995, probably two percentage points of the 69% total return. The allocations I got were very small—$2,000 to $5,000 worth of stock on a hot deal. Now, I was and will be very aggressive in buying new issues in the aftermarket, even on the day they are issued. One that I missed recently is a perfect example. Advanced Fibre Communications is a leading company in its niche that is growing leaps and bounds. I met with the company and knew it very well. The IPO filing indicated a price of $14. It actually went public at $25 and the first trade was $38. I was at a conference and gave a broker an order, which we missed. I would have bought 200,000 or 300,000 shares that day, at $38 or $40, if I'd been at my desk; unfortunately, I wasn't. Now the stock's at $57.

How much of your success is due to your trading?
A lot. I trade around core positions. Take Ascend Communications. I got shut out of the IPO but bought it aggressively in the aftermarket and have held it ever since. Ascend will go from 1.5% to 5% of the portfolio, depending on a number of things: the time of the year, how well the stock has done in the past month or three months, where it is in its product cycle, management changes, what competitors are doing. And I bought very aggressively in July, when everything was getting slammed. Ascend was in the low $40s. Now it's at $65 and I'm trimming back on it again.

Do you set target prices for selling?
No. I sort of go by feel. After a long run, when a stock seems to top out, I'll probably be lightening up.

What's going to happen to your funds in a bear market? In the dip during last May to July, Van Wagoner Emerging Growth fell three times as much as the overall market.
In a compressed bear market, where people are unloading stocks just as fast as they can, regardless of price, these funds are going to get whacked. In a bear market, stocks go down.

Garrett, you're still a one-man band. How long can you

keep this up before you collapse and they carry you out?

Years and years, because I like what I do. Actually, I took two days off around Labor Day. Before that, in 1992 sometime. Anyway, you're in our global headquarters, and you can see there's no room to build a staff.

There's not even a name on the door.

Right. But I'm negotiating new space and will bring in three or four new investment people by early 1997.

Were you a one-person operation at Govett, too?

Yes.

Are you fearful that if others share the decision-making, that whatever it is that makes your funds shine will be diluted?

I wouldn't call it a fear so much as an opportunity to bring in the right people who can help me leverage my time and keep the returns high.

I would say, though, that I don't expect to be number one or at the top of the list of funds every year. This has been—I don't want to call it a fluke, but . . .

You've been phenomenal.

Okay. But is that going to continue? I'm not going to say it will. The process I use and the process my organization will use should keep us out of the bottom, but I don't strive to be number one, nor can my funds always be number one.

And I would agree that as funds grow in size it's harder to perform. Absolutely. Running an $8 million fund is much easier than running an $800 million fund.

And if your dad came to you and asked which of your three funds his money should go into for maximum long-term gain, where would you point him?

He has asked, actually. And I told him what I'll tell you: I have one-third of my money in each fund and I'm not going to get into picking which one will do best. Dad didn't like my answer, by the way.

The elements of Garrett Van Wagoner's style: He maintains a sensitive antenna for ideas and then jumps on them fast and hard, intent on gaining insights into a company, its products, its leaders. He's not a momentum player—that is, buying stocks that are going up because they are going up. But he definitely wants earnings to be rising rapidly. And he seeks assurance that, in a flat market, he can make a lot of money on a stock over the next 12 to 18 months.

But these are the methods of a lot of growth investors. The missing ingredient here you must ascribe to art, not science. The word "intense" hardly does justice to Van Wagoner. His energy level is off the chart, which explains how he could run the Govett fund, and then three of his own, singlehandedly for four consecutive years. Couple that with the sixth sense also possessed by good journalists—a burning curiosity and urge to know everything—and you have a measure of what drives this person. Plus, there is Van Wagoner the trader, who goes in and out of core positions of stocks he knows and understands, riding the waves of the market, diving in on dips, selling on big price run ups, going with his intuitions.

It's too soon to write the real last word. His remarkable—unprecedented—record of success was achieved in an extraordinary period for the American stock market. The years 1993 through 1996 rewarded risktaking, daring and cunning, all of which Van Wagoner possesses in abundance. But this will not always be so. There will come times when all of these qualities will be punished by an unforgiving stock market. Look at Garrett Van Wagoner's long-term record after it includes more than a momentary period of adversity and you will know whether he really has the right stuff.

Ralph Wanger

In a letter to shareholders a few years ago, Acorn fund's Ralph Wanger made this observation about investing: Over time, the difference between mediocrity and outstanding achievement is having a few great ideas—in his case, three. Idea number one was to load up on Houston Oil & Minerals, an obscure exploration company, in 1973. Its value rose by a factor of 24, and it saw Wanger's young fund through the ruinous 1973–74 bear market. His second killer stock was Cray Research, which he bought in 1978 for $1.5 million and ultimately sold for $20 million. His third, in 1988, was International Game Technology—a $5-million bet that paid off twentyfold. Concluded Wanger: "It's a little bit like baseball. Babe Ruth hit a lot of home runs even though he struck out a lot. The big winners can really carry the team to victory."

That's vintage Wanger, wrapping an important observation inside a colorful metaphor. And in fact, Acorn fund (so named because it invests in small companies) has generated a total return more than twice that of the overall market since its beginning in 1970. The year 1996 promised to be the seventh of the past nine when Acorn's total return exceeded 20%.

At the time of our initial interview, in late 1994, Acorn fund had been closed to new investors for several years. More recently, Acorn International, begun in 1992 to invest in small companies overseas, had closed its doors as well. So Wanger's talents were a scarce commodity. But we sought him out in Chicago because small companies and their potential for rapid gains in the price of the stocks are a lure that investors can't seem to resist. Wanger has stuck with this specialty longer than any fund manager we are aware of. What rules—or is it metaphors?—does he invest by? (Beware: Wanger's sense of humor is desert-bone dry.)

KIPLINGER'S: Acorn is always described as a small-company growth fund. But results suggest you also look for undervalued companies. Which is it?

WANGER: Both. I've never thought of Acorn as a growth fund. Obviously, earnings growth is a nice thing. If you can find a company that is going to do a lot better in the future, you can expect that its stock will go up. But you still want to buy the stock at a reasonable price, for two reasons: First, even if high growth is going to occur, it's still worth only a certain amount of money. Second, if there's one thing that analysts do consistently, it's overestimate growth rates. They are wildly overoptimistic. It's very common to see stacks of companies they say will grow at a 20% rate. It's a nice round number that gets people excited. It should. I mean, 20% growth over a reasonable amount of time is spectacular.

I did some calculations on Wal-Mart in the early 1990s, when its revenues were growing at a 25% rate. At that pace it would have accounted for 100% of retail sales in the U.S. by the year 2015. But common sense says that growth is a self-limiting process. If you look at their records, the companies that were supposed to grow forever and dominate their industries are in many cases no longer considered to be such super companies.

Examples being?
Schlumberger, IBM, Burroughs, Polaroid.

Why did you choose to stick with small companies?
When the fund began, in 1970, there was a two-tier market. You had large companies selling at 20 times earnings, and small companies with prospects similar to large companies selling at 12 times earnings. There seemed to be a lot more value in the smaller companies, so I leaned that way. And back then there were a lot of small companies not followed by analysts. You could call on somebody and get information that had not been widely published.

Where do you find investment ideas?

Ideas come from everywhere—from Wall Street sources, from reading trade journals, from talking with a company's competitors. People in an industry know who's doing the interesting stuff.

What hurdles must a stock surmount before you will buy it?

I call my favorite test the "quit test." You find a company that excites you so much that you say, "This is so exciting and so much better than what I'm doing running a mutual fund that I'd like to quit this job, buy 100% of the company and run it." That's not practical, but sometimes people actually do it. One of the stocks we own is Systems & Computer Technology. It was followed by a nice young brokerage analyst we talked to frequently. One day he said, "I'm not going to be talking to you again as an analyst." I said, "What happened? Did you get indicted again?" And he said, "No, I'm going to work for Systems & Technology in its marketing department." I sure as heck bought more of that stock.

More realistically, every idea must pass a dividend-discount model test.

Can you explain what that means?

The test tells you what the company's potential is worth in current dollars. Its main inputs are the expected earnings-growth rate and the interest rates you have to forgo to own that stock instead of a bond. In the end, you may avoid paying 30, 40 or 50 times earnings for stocks.

Do you estimate earnings for stocks you follow?

Yes, about two years into the future. We always seem to estimate too high, too. It's a land-mine problem: If you have soldiers advancing against the enemy, chances are great that any one soldier will make it across the minefield and be an effective fighter, winning the battle. But there are mines out there, so you know you are going to lose some people—you just don't know which ones. By the same token, some of your investment ideas will get blown up and your overall performance won't be as good as you had hoped. The stocks that hit the mines will have no growth, or very disappointing growth.

The other reason for overestimating results is that the stocks you buy are the ones you're most optimistic about. There's a theory that says stock prices are set by optimists. If you think Wal-Mart's great days are over and that it won't do much over the next several years, your normal response is to ignore Wal-Mart. You won't be a factor in setting its stock price. The people who are actively buying and selling it are the ones who believe the company is doing great things. So if prices are set by optimists, it follows that you should leave room for disappointments.

Is there a stock that exemplifies your investment style?

International Game Technology has some interesting characteristics beyond the fact that its price is now 40 times what we paid for it. One is that it is in line with one of our key investment themes, which is to buy stocks that get the downstream benefits of technology. It took enormous brilliance to invent television. But the big money in TV was made by the people who owned the stations and the cable companies. All you have to do to run a cable company is get a license from the city and be mean to your customers.

IGT benefited marvelously from technology. It reinvented the humble mechanical slot machine, which inside looks like an old cash register—full of springs and cams and levers. By replacing the works with a microprocessor, IGT created something more than just an electronic slot machine. It's a new device that offers more interesting games, eliminates maintenance, allows you to get progressive jackpots or add lottery components. All of a sudden, casinos are taking out craps tables to put in more slot machines.

An IGT slot machine sells for $5,000. If the company tried to sell the same microprocessor for your kid to put inside a personal computer, it couldn't get $500 for it.

Isn't it risky to invest by metaphor—for example, in

**companies that are secondary beneficiaries of technology?
Isn't this kind of advice too vague?**

All investing is done by metaphor. Metaphors dominate our
life. Your broker calls you and says: "This is Murray. I've got a
stock here that's going to be the next Motorola, the next Intel."
That's a metaphor.

**Then how do you separate a meaningful metaphor from a
meaningless one?**

Sometimes you don't. Those land mines are out there, and you
get blown up a lot. But metaphors only give you things to look at, not
lists of stocks to run out and buy. You still have to find out if there's a
good company behind the name, who's running it and how well,
whether finances are in order, and so forth. Once in a while you find
something that's very good, and you can ride it for a while and make
enough money to make a difference.

**Speaking of riding a good stock, why is Acorn's
turnover so low?**

It goes back to investment themes. One of the problems of a
small-stock portfolio is that trading costs are very high—not only
commissions, but your effect on the price when you try to buy or sell
5% of a company. We may not be able to predict the future, but one
thing we do know is that if you keep your transaction costs down,
you're better off than if you don't. And keeping transaction costs low
means you're going to hold your stocks for a long time. Acorn has a
20% to 25% turnover rate, which means that we hold stocks four to
five years. If you are going to hold a stock that long, you need a
reason to think that the stock will do better than average over a very
long period of time.

Sometimes the reason is a niche. Harley-Davidson is an
example of a great niche company. We own it. It's the only
motorcycle maker in the United States, and the ones outside the
U.S. aren't that exciting. What you've got in Harley is maybe the
best brand name in the U.S. Coca-Cola is a good brand name, but

people don't tattoo it on their bodies.

How small a company will you buy? And how large a company?

We spend most of our time looking at companies between $60 million in stock-market value on the small side and $800 million on the large side. It's like any kind of diet: When you see something really sensational, maybe you'll go outside the range when nobody is looking. The market cap of our median holding is $350 million. Five years ago it was probably smaller.

Acorn owns an enormous number of stocks—368. Why so many?

If you're running a small-cap fund, the number of stocks you have is a direct function of the amount of money you have. If your typical stock has a market cap of $300 million, a $5-million position represents 2% of that company's value, which is a fairly large amount. Divide Acorn's $2 billion in assets by $5 million and you get 400 stocks.

That law of arithmetic is quite rigorous. The only way to take bigger positions is to buy bigger companies. By law, funds are limited to owning 10% of a company. You're also limited by liquidity and trading ability. So there are both legal and practical limits. As the fund grows, we have to either change our style and buy medium-size companies—which is certainly an available strategy—or own more stocks and look like an index fund.

When do you sell a stock?

One of the things we have on our data base is the reason we own the stock. It will say something like, "I own this stock because these guys have a new drug for multiple sclerosis that's going to make the company grow very rapidly." Now one of two things can happen. Either some hamster in the lab gets diarrhea, and the drug goes into the ashcan—at that point you should sell the stock, because the reason you bought it doesn't exist anymore—or the drug succeeds. The stock goes from $10 to $50, and then its run is over. If a stock looks like it's getting really overpriced relative to our model, we have to take a look at it.

Small-company stocks can go out of favor, too. What will happen when the next seven-year hibernation occurs?

Maybe we'll go international and buy small companies in other countries where the cycle is different. In many of the emerging markets abroad, it's like the 1960s were here—there are fewer analysts and it's easier to find a good company that's not widely followed. But there's a long cycle in small-company stocks, and I think we're still in the middle of an upswing that began in 1990.

The year 1994 is almost over, and your fund is down. What kind of year was it?

A sleeper. If on December 31, 1993, everybody had sold their stocks, put the money into Treasury bills and gone to Hawaii, today they'd have better investment results and a bad sunburn.

How do you console yourself when the numbers don't turn out well?

I go home and kick Alex, the rabbit. But I don't want to be portrayed as a rabbit abuser. We aren't having an awful year—just a flat one, like everybody else. If you had a total return of 3%, you did great. It's like a boat race: The previous three years the wind was very strong, and if you got out there and did your thing you could be up 25% or 30% in a year. Those who didn't quite catch the wind might be up 15% or 20%. Now there's a very light wind, and you fight all afternoon to advance one boat length. More metaphors!

In the final days of 1995, big news: Acorn and Acorn International were both reopening to new investors. *Kiplinger's* writer Steve Goldberg and I tracked Wanger down. He telephoned us from the top of a Colorado ski slope, where he was vacationing with wife Leah Zell, his co-manager of Acorn International. That's when I remembered how grateful I was to have interviewed Wanger in person: The man's normal voice is a whisper. "Ralph," Steve kept asking, "could you speak up a bit?" He'd try for a sentence or two, then revert to form, his voice occasionally overwhelmed by static on the phone line and by what sounded like a riverboat paddle going slap-slap-slap-slap very near his telephone mouthpiece.

It turned out that Wanger was far more excited by the prospects of Acorn International than by those of the older Acorn fund, which focuses mainly on U.S. stocks. "At this point in the market cycle there are more interesting things happening in foreign markets than in U.S. markets," he explained. "But since our shareholders can transfer money between Acorn International and Acorn, it didn't make sense to say one fund was reopening and the other remaining closed. So we reopened them both." When asked which fund he would advise his brother-in-law to invest in, Wanger replied, "Acorn International."

One reason may be that both 1994 and 1995 had been mediocre for Acorn fund. Its 1994 total return was –7.5%, when most small-company growth funds had about broken even. Then in 1995 it returned 21%, or 17 percentage points lower than the S&P 500 index. International Game Technology, Acorn's great success of recent times, had fallen in value by one third in 1995 (although its share price doubled in 1996). Harley Davidson—a low-tech stock if there ever was one—wasn't afire, either. Wanger noted that used Harley motorcycles now sell for more than new ones. "Maybe Harley ought to make used bikes," I said. Replied Wanger: "They sell every bike they make, so they maybe should make more new ones." He sounded frustrated, but Harley's shares varoomed from $26 to $45 in 1996, so that was consolation.

Any number of small-company investors will tell you that the 1990s have been trying. The market for these securities has been fickle, rewarding risk one year and punishing it the next. Technology isn't Acorn's bag—it had a normal weighting in tech-related stocks in 1995—and small-company funds not soaking up technology's cloudburst were merely so-so that year. Finally, Wanger now concedes that his talents in recent years have been spread thin. In 1995, he essentially doubled the number of people working with him to track Acorn's 340 stocks, from two to four. Reopening Acorn puts the onus on Wanger to show some renewed vigor in his oldest fund. He'll have to think harder—and come up with new metaphors.

Donald Yacktman

I don't think somebody suddenly goes from being a genius to being an idiot," says Donald Yacktman. But for the first 14 months after this highly regarded money manager went on his own in mid 1992, at the age of 50, as proprietor of the fund that bears his name, he didn't look very smart. The stock market kept going up, but returns from Yacktman fund kept going down.

All that ended in the second half of 1993, when the stock market quit going up and Yacktman fund quit going down. Since then, Yacktman's methods have worked well, as they did from 1982 to 1991, when he managed Selected American Shares. His methods can be distilled into a single statement: Buy big, growing, boring companies when they're beaten down in price and sell them when prices approach peak valuations. And his methods explain why he did so poorly at first. By definition, everything he bought for the new fund was in Wall Street's doghouse. But with the passage of time a rhythm developed and his methods were vindicated, as those big, boring growth companies began returning to favor.

Investors who pick their own stocks can learn a lot from Don Yacktman—the importance of patience, for one thing. Listen in on this mid-1995 conversation in Yacktman's Chicago office, just west of the Loop.

KIPLINGER'S: Do you know any successful investor whose stock-picking methods are pure happenstance?

YACKTMAN: No. And the more logical an investing strategy, the more likely it is to succeed.

Your own way of investing—how did it evolve?

After I'd been in this business for about ten years, I said to myself, "Yacktman, what have you learned?" There are generally two types of investors. You have growth-stock buyers and you have value buyers. I felt that growth-stock buyers tended to buy better businesses but paid too much for them. The value investors tended to buy poor-quality, lousy businesses, but because they bought and sold at good prices they made money, too.

My conclusion: Wasn't there something in between? Something that would take into account owning good businesses but buying them as undervalued stocks?

From this evolved a more structured method of stock picking. Basically, I look for good businesses run by people who are oriented toward shareholders and whose stock can be bought relatively cheaply.

By "good" businesses, don't you mean "extremely profitable" ones?

Yes. I mean companies with high returns on tangible assets. In other words, a company needs fixed assets and working capital to run its business. What I like to see is a high rate of cash generation on those assets. Staying with the most profitable businesses is the way to go.

What I basically do is calculate the cash flow—that is, earnings plus depreciation minus what's necessary to reinvest in the business—and compare that with tangible assets, which do not include such things as goodwill. I don't focus on earnings growth. Earnings growth and dividends are derivative of a company's cash-generating abilities. Nor do I put faith in anyone's estimates of future earnings growth.

No steel mills, railroads, airlines or other capital-intensive companies?

If you added up profits of the airline industry every year since Kitty Hawk, the result would be a negative number. It's a lousy business. The same with hotels. We've made 30-year comparisons because I like to own stocks a long time. In the past 30 years, Philip Morris, adjusted for splits, has gone from 33 cents to $70 per share.

But General Motors has remained virtually flat.

Are these things you can analyze from your armchair, by running the numbers?

We go right to the reports that the companies produce to get the data. Most commercial data bases lack things we want.

Your next prerequisite is "shareholder-oriented management." What does that mean?

A manager has five options for the cash that a business generates. First, you can reinvest it in the business—research and development, marketing, and so forth. After that, the good, profitable businesses usually have four options: One is to make acquisitions, which are tricky—like trading baseball players. Another is to buy back stock, and I like to see a company willing to do this, particularly on price weakness. Or you can pay down debt—which most very profitable companies don't have a lot of anyway—or increase the dividend, which I'm not especially enamored of because it's double taxation for a tax-paying shareholder.

Out of this, how do you know that a company is run with the shareholders' well-being at heart?

It's a judgment call, and more than anything it may depend on experience. You're looking at the cumulative impact of decisions that top management makes. Its job is to make new investments with the cash flow to realize high returns, just as the original business did, and thereby raise the value of the business.

The third element you look at is price. Do you want a stock that's down from its high, or what?

I want a stock that sells for much less than its private market value, which is what a rational person would pay to buy the whole company. This can sometimes be hard to figure out, but a lot of businesses transfer and sell in the open market, and you can get an idea of what the value is. Of course, it's also true that a decline in the stock price can mean a better value over the long pull.

There's a lot of fluctuation: The typical large company's stock will vary by 50% from its low to its high each year.

You've outlined a simple set of investment criteria. What's the hard part?

The big ingredient that's necessary is patience. A lot of people in our business are driven by short-term results. They may realize what they should be doing, but they use what is affectionately referred to as the momentum strategy.

Which means investing in stocks simply because they're going up, on the theory that what goes up will keep going up?

Yes. Supposedly, about 70% of investors use this, and in my mind it's a little bit of sophisticated speculation. Value investing requires not only knowledge about the company but patience as well. You must have a high degree of confidence in the businesses in which you invest. Then when they come down in price, you can build a large position. For example, when Nike sank to $50 per share, you couldn't give it away. At $76 today, everybody loves it.

You seem to follow and buy from a rather small universe of large-company stocks.

That's correct—roughly 100. Over a period of years I have, in effect, developed an internal data base. Slowly you develop your own comfort index in individual businesses that you'd love to own when the price is right. And when they reach those prices, you nail them down. The advantage to this is that even if you're wrong about these businesses, you can almost always at least break even.

The portfolio is pretty concentrated. Is that intentional?

It's a result of two things. Half of Standard & Poor's 500-stock index is not represented—the capital-intensive cyclical companies. And when one company in a high-return industry goes down, so do other companies in the same industry. So we ended up with large positions in Johnson & Johnson, Merck and Pfizer because the drug industry had fallen out of favor. The same thing happened in tobacco with Philip Morris and RJR Nabisco, and in apparel stocks with Liz Claiborne, Fruit of the Loom, Nike, Reebok and Stride Rite.

That brings up another point: Most people would instantly recognize almost every one of the 38 stocks that Yacktman fund owns. Why the emphasis on huge companies?

There's very low risk in owning large companies. It's hard to kill a company that is making profits of more than $100 million per year. Lots of little companies are single-product firms, and when they come down in price it takes more patience for them to turn around. Those we do own, such as Valassis Communications, have unbelievable economics, which is why I'm willing to buy them.

Valassis puts advertising inserts in your Sunday newspaper—those books of coupons for Quaker Oats products and so forth. It's a very profitable business and generates enormous amounts of cash. There are really only two companies in this field. When a third company tried to enter the field, the price of Valassis went down and we were buyers. Now it's a duopoly again. We bought our position at $10 per share, and now it's $17.

When do you sell a stock?

When it gets close to the private market value, I'll start to scale back. It's a function of my discomfort, I guess, and not a mechanical decision. Nobody is ever clever enough to calculate PMV exactly right. Or something else may look more compelling. Right now we're swapping Merck for Abbott Laboratory. The two had been trading at virtually the same price. Now Merck is at $70, and Abbott at less than $40. You say, "Gee, at these prices, I'd rather own Abbott."

Do you pay any attention to the direction of the stock market or what may be its future direction?

Very little, although it's interesting to talk about. What I pay most attention to is a stock's discount to the private market value. If we can buy a stock for 50% of what it's worth, that's more relevant than whether the economy is going up or down by 1% or the stock market is going up or down. The other problem is, if you start with the macro, top-down approach, there are so many decisions to make before you get down to the merits of specific stocks that it dilutes the whole process.

In retrospect, what hurt your fund's results in its first 14 months, when it was 20 percentage points behind the S&P 500 in total return?

What happened was that drug and health care stocks went to historical lows, on a relative basis. Valuations were off the bottom of the chart. That's why we had so much money in that area, and in tobacco. Again, those manic-depressive cycles!

If the drug stocks were pummeled and going nowhere and Philip Morris was under a cloud, why didn't you just sell those stocks, let the carnage continue, and buy them back when they started looking better? You'd have saved your shareholders all those losses.

It goes against the grain of everything we do. That would be speculation, as opposed to being a value buyer. In other words, those stocks were selling at their biggest discount to their real worth precisely when the pressure was the highest.

Yes, but you were suffering with them.
Only in the short term.

How can your shareholders profit from what some people might call your stubbornness, or you might call your consistency? Essentially, for two years the fund was underwater in total return?

There's a narrow difference between being stubborn and being determined. If you're right—and I was, ultimately—you're determined. The way investors should handle something like this is to add money. As it turned out, every quarter we had more money flowing into the fund than flowing out. My biggest fear then was that people would put money in, become disappointed too soon and take it all out at the wrong time. I didn't want to see anybody hurt. I don't think many were.

During that time, did you reexamine your own methods and make changes in your investment methods?

Over the years I've always tried to focus and improve what I do. Sure, at times like that you reassess and ask if there are things you could do better. But any mistakes I made were minor. The big problem was to have a new fund with the methods I employ. The stocks we buy are on J curves. We buy them on the left side of the J, and then hopefully they climb the right-hand side. But when you start with all cash and buy things that are out of favor, they don't suddenly go into favor, especially in a rising market like we had then.

You're a Mormon, aren't you?

Yes. Are you going to ask about tobacco stocks?

Yes. Doesn't it bother you at all owning a Philip Morris?

Well, yes and no. I don't own any tobacco stocks personally. But my job is to find the most profitable businesses at the cheapest prices, and tobacco companies hit the matrix. This is a public mutual fund, not my personal portfolio. If it were my money I would do as I want. When I run public money I must be objective, and this means those stocks are in the fund.

How do you want to be judged as a fund manager?

Compare us to the S&P 500—or, since you can't buy that index, to something like the Vanguard Index 500 fund. We hope to beat the S&P by three or four percentage points. Look at this fund after it's been around five years, in mid 1997. We're still behind, but the race is not over. After all, this is a marathon, not a sprint.

Don Yacktman and his fund are unusual in this respect: He's a value investor but his fund isn't a value fund. Value investors buy stocks that sell at a substantial discount to their real worth, however that is calculated. Value permeates Yacktman's view of the investment landscape, and by his own admission he pays no attention to earnings-growth rates. Yet, lo and behold, when you look at what his fund owns and how it behaves, what you see is the quintessential large-company growth fund, whose stocks are all experiencing good, consistent earnings growth. So investors in this fund should think growth, not value.

Clearly, Yacktman's buy-'em-when-they're-down stock-picking method hurt the fund early on because initially all his stocks were down. Moreover, they stayed down a long time. Yacktman fund's returns for the three years from October 1993 are probably a better indicator of future performance—great versus the S&P 500 in flat or down markets, okay to slightly trailing in up markets—and in fact Yacktman outreturned the S&P 500 by an annualized 1.5 percentage points. Another clue to future performance: his track record running Selected American Shares from 1983 until early 1992. During that period, Selected's total return beat the S&P 500 by one percentage point on an annualized basis.

The Switch Hitters & Niche Hitters

Bing Carlin

Jerome Dodson

Daniel Fuss

Kenneth Heebner

Michael Hirsch

Brad Lewis

As a group these are the most interesting investors to be found in this book. They're lumped together because calling them growth or value people doesn't really get to the heart of what they do. One of them doesn't even own stocks, another invests only in other mutual funds, and a third buys what his black box tells him to.

Julian (Bing) Carlin (IAI Regional) is really an earnings-growth chaser. But he shows up here because his approach to investing—concentrating on companies headquartered within a day's drive of his hometown—is quite unusual. You can't do that everywhere. How many companies are within a day's drive of Wichita or Tampa, and can you construct a powerful portfolio from the ones you do find? Carlin, a gregarious and social fellow who claims to do some of his research by talking to business executives on the golf course and in the hunting blind, is fortunate to hail from Minneapolis, which is one the nation's hotbeds of venture capital.

Jerome Dodson (Parnassus) is at heart a value investor, but what sets him apart from the others in this collection of interviews is his insistence that the companies he invests in pass his tests of social responsibility. Apart from that, Dodson runs a concentrated portfolio—not many stocks, but a lot invested in each of those he chooses. This tends to make the fund's results either very impressive or very unimpressive, and Dodson has known both of these extremes.

My associate Manuel Schiffres said it couldn't be done—that *Kiplinger's* couldn't cobble together a readable interview with a bond picker of such obtuse opinions as Daniel Fuss (Loomis Sayles Bond). Well, it was nip and tuck. A time or two I was lost in space trying to comprehend what Dan was saying, and Manny had to come in with a question that got the interview back on track. The result is readable, all right, and I recommend it to all stock investors who think owning bonds is dullsville.

Kenneth Heebner (CGM Capital Development and CGM Mutual) is a switch hitter. He can be a growth investor today and a value investor tomorrow. Perhaps it's more accurate to state that his funds are part growth, part value—the approach depending on his own analysis in each particular case. It's fair to say that Heebner does a bit of top-down analysis of the economy, and this enters into his stock selection, too. His ability to think strategically is probably the distinguishing characteristic of his style.

Michael Hirsch (FundManager funds) comes at investing differently from all the others. He invests in other mutual funds on behalf of his shareholders. He knows just about everyone in the business worth knowing, and brings to his job some deeply felt opinions about putting together a portfolio of funds. I don't share them all, but it's also true that he has made me change the way I think about some things—international investing, for instance.

Finally, Brad Lewis (Fidelity Disciplined Equity) invests without knowing why. How could that be? He has programmed a personal computer to sort through billions of bits of data— economic stuff, market stuff, stock-price histories, and so forth—

and find relationships between events or trends and prices of individual stocks. The computer then spits out a list of stocks to buy and stocks to sell. And he does what it tells him to do. The beauty of this approach is that it actually works, and works very well, most of the time.

Bing Carlin

His 14 years as a stockbroker for PaineWebber convinced Julian (Bing) Carlin that an inquisitive investor could make as much money as he or she ever needed by picking stocks of companies headquartered within 20 miles of his hometown of Minneapolis. This isn't as preposterous as it might seem to those not familiar with the Upper Midwest. The Twin Cities area is one of the great venture-capital centers of America, on a par with California's Silicon Valley and Massachusetts's Route 128 corridor. So in 1979 Carlin put his beliefs to the test, by starting a fund that would put 80% of its money into stocks of companies based in the upper Midwest—from Wisconsin westward to Montana, from North Dakota southward to Iowa.

IAI Regional (called North Star Regional until 1987) was a smashing success and greatly enhanced Bing Carlin's reputation as a master stock picker. Every year from 1985 through 1991, the total return of IAI Regional equaled or exceeded that of Standard & Poor's 500-stock index. Clearly, geographical restrictions weren't hindering the fund. Moreover, Carlin's methods serve as a powerful incentive to kitchen-table stock pickers: Buy the things you know best. Of course, Carlin can hobnob with chairmen of these companies on the golf course and perhaps you cannot. But you can observe what you see in retail stores, as well as in your own business and in the industry of which it is a part.

The autumn of 1992 found us in the offices of Investment Advisers Inc., in Minneapolis, to find out just how Carlin does his thing.

KIPLINGER'S: When you look at IAI Regional's portfolio, the first thing that jumps out is the cash position—23% of assets. Are you awaiting the stock market's Final Reckoning?

CARLIN: No. It has a lot to do with the growth of the fund. We had $220 million in assets at the start of 1991 and $440 million at the start of 1992. Today the fund is at $580 million.

I have a pretty strict charter: to keep 80% of equity assets in the seven-state region—Wisconsin, Minnesota, North and South Dakota, Iowa, Nebraska and Montana. If the values aren't there as I perceive them, I refuse to just throw money at the market. Nor do I make calls on the market. For example, I don't say, "The market stinks. I'm going to 40% cash." I use a bottom-up approach, stock by stock.

We detect some caution on your part about stock prices.

I'm not really looking for a big correction. Back in the fall of 1990, one-third of the stocks we follow were cheap, cheap, cheap; another third were cheap, cheap; and the rest were merely undervalued. It wasn't hard to make money then. You just bought. Today, I'd call stocks in my universe slightly overpriced.

And just what is your "universe"?

Basically it's the Ninth Federal Reserve District. The stock-market capitalization of companies based in those seven states is more than $150 billion. Take away the Dakotas and Montana, which have $3 billion among them, and it comes down to $90 billion in Minnesota, $27 billion in Wisconsin, $20 billion in Nebraska and $12 billion in Iowa—some 250 companies in all.

What would it take for your fund to become fully invested?

I go stock by stock—targeting individual companies at a precise price. For instance, if I saw Honeywell go back to $62 a share, I'd commit another $6 million. It's at $65 now, and I have 100,000 shares. I could double up very easily. You could start blowing $6 million or $12 million at a crack.

I'd do the same with General Mills if the price were right. Medtronic has been a great stock, and I could add more.

Other regional stock funds have been mostly duds. What made this one different?

You can't be a good fisherman by fishing in the YMCA swimming pool. You need a trophy lake holding trophy fish. That's what we have—a diverse group of companies, and lots of them. Within 100 miles of where we sit, there's $80 billion of stock capitalization.

Second, you need growth characteristics. Third, you need a technology base. We had computer technology in Control Data and Honeywell, and it spread into medical-device companies in the region. There's a lot of venture capital out here. And new companies just keep bubbling up.

How do you select stocks? Do you employ any particular method?

I believe in doing three things. One, go out and talk to the companies—meet the managers and see the place. I've talked to managers of about 70% of the stocks that IAI Regional owns. In the next year I want to talk to all of them again. Two, get the numbers. Three, have a high degree of awareness of what's going on in your community—who's doing well and who isn't. That comes from networking and takes time to develop.

Describe how this process works in real life.

Take Medtronic. It makes heart valves. We like stocks that are part of the solution to medical-cost problems, which Medtronic is. You've got to have pricing power, too, which Medtronic has: The alternative to a heart valve is that you die, so I'll take one. You have all the ingredients here—wind at their back, demographics, pricing power.

They're located in our backyard. We happen to manage money for their pension fund. So we went over and looked at the company. We met their distributors and the doctors who use their products—the specialists at Mayo Clinic [in nearby Rochester, Minnesota]. We did all sorts of cross-checks.

We concluded that Medtronic will be huge in the 1990s. Everything is going right for it—it's one hell of a company. Last spring, when you could buy the stock for under $35, you just backed the truck in and loaded up. [This stock's price has been adjusted to account for a subsequent split.]

Is Medtronic the sort of stock you buy and hold?

I try to always own companies like this—a minor or major position, often depending on the price. Medtronic is now at $50, up from $35 in a month's time, and I may elect to sell some of it. On the other hand, I don't usually abandon a company like this or a Dayton Hudson or a General Mills. Maybe Dayton Hudson is not doing well because consumers are not doing well. So I might have less than a full position. But if I see Dayton Hudson's price go under $60, I'll go for it.

How do you decide when to sell?

I decide a couple of ways. One is to sit down and ask what a stock should sell for versus the overall market—the S&P 500. Using Medtronic, say I decide that a company with all of its wonderful characteristics should sell at a 50% premium to the market. Then I have to decide what the market will sell for 18 months down the road. Maybe I conclude the market will sell for 15 times earnings. That makes Medtronic fully priced at a price-earnings ratio of 22. If they're going to earn $2.50 a share 18 months from now, then my target is $55 a share.

Maybe that's high, maybe that's low. But it's what I shoot for. When that price gets close, I'll start to sell—20,000 shares here, 20,000 there. I can't sell all at once when the bell rings—not when I own 150,000 shares.

And the other reason you sell?

When something goes wrong. I don't believe that hope belongs to loser stocks. If bad stuff goes on with a large company, I cut back. If it's a little company, I take no prisoners. I just get out.

Do many good ideas come to you at odd moments?

Actually, some of the best ones come when I'm out and about. I own a place up north. It's about three miles from Grand Casino Mille Lacs, which is on Chippewa reservation land. The casino management company is publicly owned and splits profits 40-60 with the Chippewas. More casinos will be opened, too. I went there, saw what was happening and said to myself, "I want to get on the other side of the table!" Grand Casinos Inc. was at $5 or so, and I bought some. Then I drove past there in October '91, when we were buried in a 28-inch snowstorm, and the place was packed. It was packed again last February, when the temperature was 20 below. So I just kept buying. It went up to $24, and I scaled back. I mean, it's going to earn maybe $1.20 a share in the fiscal year ending July '93, and is a gambling stock worth a P/E of 20? If they screw up, Minnesota will jerk the license. When the stock went down, I bought in again at $12. Now it's at $17, and I'm starting to scale back again. I sold 70,000 shares at $16.50 and another 30,000 a few minutes ago at $17.

You also run IAI Stock fund, which can invest anywhere. Its total return hasn't been impressive. Why is that?
I took it over in May of 1991 after the death of Dick Tschudy, who headed the firm and managed that fund. Dick's style was more toward income than capital growth. I tried to maneuver the assets more toward growth. But my timing was terrible because I did so just at the time that investors cooled on growth stocks and moved to cyclicals. So long as income is a priority—and that's in the prospectus—I can't compete with the Janus Twenties of this world on total return.

However, IAI Regional has done well for so long that it's hard to find a dry spell. But you underperformed the market badly in 1983 and 1984. What went wrong then?
Small-company stocks peaked in 1983, and through 1984 they were real doggies. I didn't change my style, then or ever. I didn't feel that what I was doing was wrong—only that the small-cap stocks I liked were out of favor. All I could do was keep trying to understand the companies up here.

IAI Regional lags the S&P this year. Are you frustrated now?
Not really. The 1990s are going to be like the 1970s. It was hard to make money then. The market won't deliver compounded 18% gains as it has. You'll see lower rates of return because economic growth won't be the same, and our standard of living will come down,

both relatively and absolutely. So you're going to have to focus on companies that can generate sales growth while keeping their costs under control; they won't be able to raise prices like they once did.

At the start of 1996, Carlin, then age 60, turned over IAI Regional to his assistant and co-manager of the previous two years, Mark Hoonsbeen. "I was managing $4 billion, of which IAI Regional was a part," he explained when we spoke again in 1996. "That was almost half of the equity money in the firm, and God forbid if anything had happened to me. So I began a gradual phaseout, and by 1995 I was back to just running Regional. Then I simply decided enough was enough and bagged it."

We spoke about events subsequent to the 1992 interview and their impact on IAI Regional. From that conversation:

KIPLINGER'S: You expanded the scope of IAI Regional to include Illinois. Why?

CARLIN: It's right next to Wisconsin, and we were doing a lot of work on companies headquartered there, anyway, so Illinois wasn't virgin territory. Had we not added Illinois, the market capitalization of companies in our region would have grown since 1992 from $80 billion to $200 billion. With Illinois, it's now $700 billion.

Were you driven to this decision because of all the new money invested in Regional?

Oh, yes. Because of the high flow of cash into the fund, I had to take such big positions that I had no exit strategy—no way to sell one in a hurry. That's what is happening to a lot of guys today—buying big quantities of illiquid stocks, which is fine when the price goes up. I also wanted the opportunity to invest a little more in Illinois companies.

Meanwhile, starting in 1992, the total returns of Regional didn't look quite as good, did they?

That's when we went big time—the money just poured in, and we had no good targets of opportunity. That was just before we added Illinois. So we ended 1992 with a return of 3.5%, versus 7.5% for the S&P. The next year, 1993, we were up 9% and the S&P 10%, but a lot of guys did 20% and we ended up in the third quartile of long-term-growth funds. Then in 1994 we about tied the S&P by just breaking even, and in 1995 we gained 32% and trailed the S&P by five percentage points.

You must have been disappointed with 1995.

Well, our highest year-to-date return was the last trading day of the year, so I finished at my best. I was underweighted in technology, and most of that was in medical-technology stocks. We didn't own any semiconductor stocks and there are no big software companies in our region. But look, a lot of the funds that did best were taking huge risks. Even Fidelity Magellan had 43% of assets in technology stocks at one time in 1995. Its return for the year of 36% is commendable, but not so commendable when you take risk into consideration.

Didn't adding Illinois sort of dilute your specialized knowledge about an area, Minnesota, that had given you a special leg up in the past?

I had that edge. But you win with a portfolio by sort of indexing to the overall market and then taking big bets with four or five companies that might be 10% or 15% of your assets. In most portfolios, 85% of what you own is noise—stocks that cancel each other out. But that other 15%, if you don't have any losers among them—bingo! It's payday!

Aren't you more likely to find "bingo!" stocks in the North Country than in Chicago, where everybody else is looking?

In general, you are absolutely right. I screwed up on a few stocks. Northwest Airlines stock went crazy in 1995 and I should have been in it, but I don't think much of its chairman and passed it up. U.S. Robotics was a huge winner. We passed on it because we didn't think we had enough intelligence on it. That's one we missed, too. But generally if I rate a management well, 80% to 90% of the time the stock performs well. You get to know these guys. You see these guys socially. You play golf with them. You go fishing with them. This is a small community, when you think about it. You hear what's going on—what's good, what's bad. This is what I'm going to do now.

What? Are you starting a new fund?

No. It's a real small thing. Some of the people my age came to me with family money. Basically, what I'm going to do is invest it for them in what I consider some of the best companies in the world, but put 35% to 40% of the equity in companies located right here in the Twin Cities. I'm not even going to Wisconsin. I'm talking about the new health care companies here—the ones with exciting things that could turn out to be the next Sci-Med Life Systems. We'll take ten or 15 of these companies and put them into the portfolio—kind of a publicly traded venture-capital group. That's kind of fun to do, because I'll have the time.

I also asked Carlin during that 1996 interview what had happened to Grand Casino Mille Lacs, which operated the casino on the Chippewa reservation. He says he traded out of the stock the last time at $33. "It's one of the few gambling stocks that has hung in there pretty good. We did well on it. But the trouble with gambling stocks is that every time they go down, some shareholders start complaining, 'You shouldn't own companies like that.' But if you make a lot of money on it, nobody says a thing."

And where was Medtronic, the stock so beloved by Carlin in 1992? It was MIA in the portfolio of IAI Regional. "We sold it at $60," Carlin replied. "I suggested to Mark that he keep a core position in companies like that, but when it traded for 30 times earnings he just couldn't resist selling. I told him the other day, with the stock down to $49, that he ought to get back in—this is one of the great medical-device companies of the world!" Obviously, our man Bing is having a hard time letting go.

Jerome Dodson

Socially conscious funds are known for delivering substandard returns—a reputation that they well deserve. In that environment, Jerome Dodson stands apart. The founder and portfolio manager of Parnassus fund demonstrated, for a while at least, that you can do very well indeed while doing good.

Early on, his fund was almost unimaginably bad. Dodson, born in 1943, came to the stock-fund business in 1984 with a background in the U.S. foreign service and experience running a socially conscious money-market fund, Working Assets. But he had never picked stocks for a living, and through 1990 his inexperience showed. Parnassus ranked 187th in five-year total return among 197 long-term-growth funds, according to Micropal Inc.

Then something happened to dramatically alter the fund's performance. For the next five years, to August 1, 1995, the fund ranked as the tenth best in the long-term-growth category.

That's when I first spoke to Dodson, in his fourth-floor office above lower California Street in San Francisco. My curiosity was aroused. What was Dodson doing that managers of other socially conscious funds were not? And just what is that nebulous, subjective practice known as socially conscious investing? I began by playing devil's advocate.

KIPLINGER'S: Why make the process of investing—difficult enough to begin with—even more dicey by layering on non-financial criteria?

DODSON: Most of our shareholders are philosophically in tune with the social factors. They like to invest in companies that are good corporate citizens. Also, if it's possible for our shareholders to persuade companies to make changes, even at the margins, they like that aspect as well.

Isn't it enough that a company abide by the law and look out for the interests of its shareholders?

That's certainly important. But there are legal products that we consider harmful to society. Tobacco is a good example. Alcohol is another. Nuclear power and weapons-contracting are also legal businesses. But our shareholders do not want to invest in those kinds of companies.

What's so bad about supplying our army? This isn't a perfect world. Don't our weapons protect this society?

It is necessary to have a strong America, and a certain amount of defense spending will always be needed. Our policy made more sense a decade ago, when I felt that military spending was overdone. I guess the easiest way to put it is that we just don't want to be part of the armaments business, even if it is a necessary business.

The strictures you named are easy to abide by—a company either does or doesn't make guns or cigarettes or nuclear power. What are the other criteria you apply?

The general areas we look at are treatment of employees, environmental protection, equal employment opportunity, community relations and, lastly, a catchall category you could label ethical business practices. There are a lot of subjective distinctions made.

Would you invest in a company that's a good corporate citizen in towns where it is active but that is vigorously anti-union?

Some of the best companies do not have unions. It's hard to unionize a company that treats employees well. Federal Express is an example. As long as a company doesn't violate the National Labor Relations Act by illegal union-busting, I don't see a problem.

What about WMX Technologies, owner of Waste Management? Its business—of disposing of trash and waste— means it will inevitably run afoul of some environmental laws.

Can you accept that?

I have a different view of WMX than yours. Although it has improved its record, there are enough other environmental companies to invest in that haven't been cited for serious pollution violations. One is Groundwater Technology. It does such things as clean up leakage from storage tanks at gasoline stations.

The criteria you use aren't set in stone, are they?

Absolutely not. It's attitude as well as a pattern of behavior that is important to us. Two cases in point are Sun Co.—the Sunoco gasoline brand—and H.B. Fuller, a chemical company. Both have been cited for minor environmental violations—as perhaps Groundwater has—as an unavoidable consequence of being in the businesses they are in. On the other hand, in our opinion, WMX deliberately violated environmental regulations.

What do you say to someone who agrees with most of what you do but vehemently disagrees with parts—for example, someone who has a deep conviction that coal has killed thousands of miners through mine explosions and black lung disease, whereas nuclear power has killed no Americans?

I tell them that maybe Parnassus fund is not for them. This same kind of thing comes up with animal testing.

Animal-rights activists have strongly felt views.

And what we tell them is that if a company experiments with animals in order to develop medical procedures that will save human lives, then we would invest in such companies. But if testing is done for cosmetics research, we would not. Of course, most animal-rights people write back to say that's not good enough for them.

What about a company like Ben & Jerry's?

It would meet the social tests, but not the financial ones. That company has two classes of shares, with weighted voting, which we tend to avoid. Also, for a long time the stock price was too high.

Couldn't the argument be made that Ben & Jerry's makes unhealthy, high-fat, high-cholesterol ice cream and therefore is not a socially responsible company?

You aren't the first person to bring that up. It does bother us, because getting people to eat high-fat ice cream is a concern.

Would you disagree with a characterization that Parnassus has a left-of-center agenda?

I would absolutely disagree. We're not an ideological fund. We apply social values and try to make a difference. A lot of this fund's shareholders are relatively conservative. They espouse family values and lean to the right on issues such as pornography, for example. We get a lot of investors who just like the fund for its family values or for religious reasons.

Make no mistake: Our investors want to make money just like anybody else. I've noticed that the flow of new money into the fund depends upon our performance. The thing is, our investors want to make money in a socially responsible way.

Speaking of performance, it hasn't always been terrific, to put it mildly. What was going on during the 1980s? Were you getting on-the-job training as a stock picker?

The fund was very erratic back then. In 1988 Parnassus was one of the top funds, so don't make it seem worse than it was. But there were three or four reasons we didn't do well in those years. First, we didn't pay enough attention to debt loads of companies we invested in. I am much more conscious now of how well a company can service its debt. Second, we didn't pay enough attention to where companies stood in their business cycle.

You were buying stocks on their way down—and they stayed down?

Yes. Most industries develop a cycle, and you want to pay attention to where a business is in its cycle, or you'll buy too soon, as we were doing. And related to that, we made the mistake of not paying attention to prospects for earnings. Earnings estimates are so notoriously unreliable that you really can't depend upon them. But you should at least know the general direction of a company's earnings.

So you made these course corrections in your investment methods. Is this why Parnassus has done so well since 1990? Or did the undervalued stocks you like to invest in simply come back into favor?

Half of each. With the exception of about 18 months from 1985 through 1990, the market was driven by stocks of large companies with steadily growing earnings. We tend to invest in small- to medium-size companies that are undervalued according to financial ratios we track. Starting in 1991, those small-company value stocks came back into favor and stayed there until this year. Now large companies and technology stocks are driving the market, almost exclusively, and this isn't helping us.

Yes, you're near the bottom so far in 1995 among long-term-growth funds.

And the thing is, last year we had 45% of assets in technology stocks. Had we not sold them as their prices rose, we'd be right up there this year.

You considered all these technology stocks undervalued last year, but not now?

Yes. That's why we are not as much in technology as we were.

What are the financial yardsticks you use to determine whether a stock is undervalued?

Ratio number one is price to book value. We prefer to buy at or below book value, but we will go as high as 150% of book value, and for a company that has hidden values or a high rate of profit growth, two times book value.

Second, we'll never pay more than 70% of a company's highest price during the past five years.

Third is price to sales—price divided by sales per share. For a normal company, we want that ratio to be no more than 0.4.

Fourth, price divided by earnings per share—the P/E ratio—should be no more than ten to 15 times earnings.

The fifth ratio is relatively new and is a measure used by Warren Buffett: Take net income after taxes, add back depreciation and amortization, and subtract capital spending and additions to working capital. What you get is free cash flow. We then project for ten years what that will be and discount the result by 9% each year, which is the minimum return we could accept, after taxes. If the result is 35% to 50% more than the price, then we consider the stock undervalued.

Do you require that all five ratios be favorable before you buy?

No. Only once in a blue moon does that happen, which is why you have to be flexible and not let a computer make your decisions.

Have you ever wondered why so many socially conscious funds have such pedestrian records?

Yes. I don't think it has anything to do with the social criteria. Rather, their financial discipline has not been effective enough. I invest from a universe of 200 companies whose financial and social facts I know well, and my fund has done well the past five years. So I don't think the social criteria of the fund are a limiting factor. Clearly, these funds need to get better at financial analysis, and then they'll do well.

I can say this because, for a number of years, Parnassus's performance was the same as all the other social funds. But rather than accepting that it had to be this way because of the social factors we consider, we began researching the companies better, got to know them better, and it made all the difference in the world. You don't need to suck wind because you're a social investor.

That was August of 1995. That month and in four of the next five, Parnassus had negative returns, including a huge 9% loss in

October and a 5% fall in December. For all of 1995—the best year for stocks in more than three decades—Parnassus merely broke even, returning less than 1%. The substandard performance continued throughout 1996. It was as if Dodson had steered his fund into a tree. Ouch!

Dodson's letter to shareholders early in 1996 read like war correspondence. The fund's three largest holdings as of June 30, 1995, were torpedoed in the second half of the year. Genus, which makes semiconductor equipment and was the fund's number-one holding, was down only 6% for the year but had fallen 41% from its June 30 price. Apple Computer (number two) was off 18% in 1995, and Toys "R" Us (number three), 25%. On and on went Dodson's amazing tale of investment casualties. Sunrise Medical (seventh-biggest holding) revealed that a division had been falsifying its sales for some time, and the stock fell 33% in 1995. CML Group (11th) was off by about half for the year, and Advanced Micro Devices (19th) dropped 34%. Concluded a chastened (but commendably candid) Dodson: "I seem to have picked every technology company that had a bad year."

I returned to Dodson in 1996 to ask whether he suspected that a pattern of investment mistakes was occurring. Or was it just a run of bad luck all at once? "It's primarily the latter," he replied. "When you have a poor year like 1995, you always do soul-searching. I could see my mistakes with great clarity in 1990. Yet I don't think I did anything terrible in 1995. I used the same methods as in the prior four years."

One thing he had *not* done, I noted, was unload his losers. Every one of the stocks mentioned above remained in the portfolio going into 1996: Genus ("there is still a lot of value in the company"), Apple ("the price will be substantially higher in the future"), Toys "R" Us ("it should make us look much better in years to come"), Sunrise ("I still think there's value in the stock"), CML Group ("should make substantial gains") and Advanced Micro ("we'll enjoy good gains in the years to come"). These are all quotes lifted right out of his shareholder report. The fact is, I told Dodson, you still like all these turkeys! "Yeah, I like them," he said. "Apple is a question, because of its mismanagement in 1995. But of the ones mentioned in the report, I haven't decided to cut bait on any of them. I think they're going to bounce back. I am, however, going over the entire portfolio to ask if there are better uses for my money."

Well, then, what did he wish he had done differently in 1995? "I'm not sure," Dodson replied, "other than to have sold off those companies earlier in the year and bought 'em back later on." Not a bad response! In fact, what Dodson did as 1996 progressed was to require that stocks Parnassus owned have a plausible chance of returning to investor favor within a year's time. On that basis, out went CML Group by mid 1996; Sunrise Medical was substantially sold, too.

The rise and subsequent fall of Parnassus fund is a lesson for us all. For all the data and information and computer power expended by today's army of portfolio managers, investing remains art, not science. Every so often, we are condemned to look at the wreckage of our best-laid plans and wonder: How could things have gotten so screwed up?

Daniel Fuss

S omeone once compared bond funds to sausage—you're better off never asking how either is made. Even so, we asked Daniel Fuss in 1996 how he made Loomis Sayles Bond fund the standout high-quality corporate-bond fund of the 1990s, and I'm glad we did. This fund's record is phenomenal. Begun in mid 1991, it delivered the second-highest total returns in its category in both 1992 and 1993, and the third-highest in 1995. (The year 1994 was another story, but more on that later.) Altogether, its track record since its founding blows away all its peers—no competitor comes even close. And the fund's yield has been at the top of the charts. It doesn't get much better than this. Daniel Fuss is becoming known as the best bond picker in America.

Fuss, born in 1933, is also the largest shareholder in this fund (less than $420 million in assets in 1996), as well as head of the bond department of Loomis Sayles and manager of a second no-load fund, Managers Bond. So when he says—as he does repeatedly in this interview—that he enjoys seeing interest rates go up and the value of his fund shares go down, you have to wonder why he is so cavalier about his own money. I went to Boston and found out.

In person, the man possesses a penetrating wit. But there's no denying Fuss is a hard-core bond junkie. He reminds me of my Uncle Phil, a professor emeritus of agricultural economics at a major midwestern university. Uncle Phil, now in his ninth decade, still pulls from his breast pocket a handwritten table of farmland values in every county of Iowa and Minnesota for each of the past 20 years. In other words, he knows the stuff that matters. Like Uncle Phil, Dan Fuss is a bit professorial. And he knows his stuff.

KIPLINGER'S: Are you seeking the highest total return possible or the highest yield? Right now you're getting both.

FUSS: My goal is to have income, per dollar of original

investment, increase a bit each year. In 1995 I could not, because interest rates fell from 8% to 6% and did so in a hurry.

But who cares? The fund's total return was 32%.

People who need income care. When rates go down, the total return looks great because the bonds appreciate in value. But I'm trying to protect the income level. As those bonds mature or are called [redeemed early] I must reinvest my profits at lower rates of interest, for lower yield. Plus, as rates go down there's great temptation by people who issue the debt to get rid of it. Everyone sees this when homeowners refinance their mortgages. Not as obvious is what happens on the corporate side. Bonds that are seemingly protected against a call are discovered to have other ways of being redeemed.

In other words, higher-yielding bonds you intended to own many more years suddenly are taken away?

Yes. The latest instance is that some of the Entergy subsidiaries are considering taking advantage of a clause in their first-mortgage bonds. The clause says that if they replace or fail to maintain their physical plant, they have to give the bondholders back their money. They say part of their plant wears out and is replaced all the time, so therefore they can repay the bonds and borrow again at lower rates.

This is all perfectly legal. The only surprise is that somebody actually thought of it, and now can you imagine another regulated utility in Texas not doing this, too? If they don't the regulators will be all over them for squandering the ratepayers' money to pay those capitalists. So here we go again.

You've said, perhaps in a moment of indiscretion, that you like to see interest rates go up. Isn't that contrary to the interests of your shareholders?

Not if rates go up in the normal course of events, because soon enough they'll go back down. Look, if inflation is taking off for the moon, no bond manager can help you. In that event, don't own bonds at all, or if you do, get into the shortest maturities possible and hope you can recoup part of your capital. Bonds can do a reasonable job only in a fairly stable environment.

So if it's in the normal course of events—interest rates going up and going down—you can capture a higher yield when rates go up. Plus, fewer bonds get called because it is less advantageous to the issuers.

How did your shareholders feel in 1994, when rates roared and their total return—yield minus the loss of value of the bonds—was −4%?

I'm sure some didn't greet it as good news. But had they asked, I'd have pointed out that their income dividend was rising. There's no such thing as a "growth" bond, in which the issuer comes back and boosts the interest rate—that is, unless it is part of the original contract. If I wanted to invest for total return with just a bit of income, I'd run a growth-and-income stock fund. So how are you going to make money in bonds? By finding bonds that are cheap relative to similar ones and that pay an above-average yield. Then someday those bonds mature or you sell them and make a profit, too. With interest rates going up as well as down, this is far easier to do.

But if I want a nice income, can't I sell a few shares at the higher price to make up for the lost income?

You certainly can. And if you identify the low point of interest rates for a long time, sell all your shares! Otherwise, if you sell some here and there and rates go lower still, you've paid taxes and you'll reinvest at lower rates that provide less income, which may be good for you because it will cause you to lose interest in the material world.

No thanks. With rates this low, is it also hard to find the sorts of bonds you prefer?

It is. We're basically buyers of discounted bonds. So when you get interest rates like this relative to where they've been the past 20 years, you ask yourself, "Where are the bargains?"

How do you go about assembling a portfolio?

I keep in mind the first principle I was taught in this business, by the president of a Wisconsin bank, who looked at me one day after a long conversation and said, "Dan, you just don't get it—we only buy bonds that go up." Good lesson for me. I don't ever know what the bond market will do. So I look at bonds individually, from the bottom up, with some top-down assumptions.

Are your assumptions about the direction of interest rates?

Not so much that as what's happening in the political sphere. How New Zealand resolves its budget debate is a very major bet for us right now. I can buy U.S. Treasury debt without doing a lot of tire kicking. But you have to evaluate the credit of British Columbia, whose bond ratings would be higher but for the fact that there is a less-stable national government.

How do you know if a bond is undervalued?

It's an intuitive process. Imagine standing on a street corner and observing everything that happens, day after day. After a while you get an intuition for things. The primary reason I will buy a bond is that it offers more yield than a U.S. Treasury bond or other comparable bonds. Then you adjust for all sorts of things, such as the fact that Treasuries aren't subject to state income taxes and for differences in credit quality. At the end of this process, you say, "I think this bond looks cheap." In fact, the reason it is cheap may be simply because a lot of the issue is for sale.

A case of supply overwhelming demand?

It's very normal to own half of a single issue of corporate bonds. Then all of a sudden a state pension fund, for example, decides it wants to sell it all, and there's no outstanding bid from a buyer. If it's a Weyerhauser 7¼% bond, maybe no one feels comfortable owning a lot of it right now. That's where we might come in. Let's say the Weyerhauser would normally yield one percentage point more than a Treasury bond of comparable maturity. But now it is offered at a price to yield 1.3 percentage points more because the seller wants out. I'd probably pass on a spread one-tenth of a percentage point above normal. But three-tenths? You get more yield and if the price ever rises to what you feel is fair value, a capital gain.

Which raises a question: When do you sell a bond?

The main part of what we do is buy bonds like the one I just described, and when they revert to normal pricing, sell. Two and a half years is our typical holding period.

The average maturity of bonds you own is very long—19 years. Your fund should have been flattened in 1994, when interest rates spiked upward so suddenly and drove down the prices of long-term bonds very steeply. Why not? Were you hyperdiversified?

There were some short-term bonds—not a lot. The fund's busted convertibles didn't get treated too badly, and a couple actually went up in price.

What's a "busted convertible"?

Bond managers love to use all their obscure terms; we're like engineers. A busted convertible is a bond that can be converted into stock if the stock rises to a designated price—except that the stock was torpedoed and there's no conversion value, meaning that the bond trades simply as a bond.

Sinker bonds—ones whose issuer is required to buy back on a regular basis from a sinking fund—cushioned the downside, too.

Why?

Because when a company is required to buy bonds at face value in a falling market, those bonds won't go down much. We had some adjustable-rate preferreds, and their interest rates readjust upward when interest rates rise.

So it was a mishmash. You had all these countervailing assets, and it decreases your sensitivity to the market.

Knowing all this—knowing your portfolio holds foreign bonds, busted convertibles, sinkers, junk bonds and undervalued investment-grade bonds—can you accurately predict how this amalgamation will react to a given change in interest rates?

In general, yes.

Did your fund behave in 1994 as you thought it should?

In my opinion, yes. In Morningstar Mutual Funds' opinion, no. Morningstar thought the fund should have done twice as badly as it did. We don't "model" well.

What's the difference between Loomis Sayles Bond and Managers Bond funds?

It comes out in one area. Managers Bond is a pure long-term, investment-grade bond fund.

No junk bonds or busted convertibles and the like?

Very little. As a result, the degree of nonmarket-relatedness diminishes greatly.

Who is Managers Bond best suited for?

For somebody allocating his assets who wants market ups and downs with somewhat more than a market yield.

And who is Loomis Sayles Bond best suited for?

For someone with at least a five-year time horizon. If you have to pay college tuition with the money in three years, don't invest in this fund.

What defensive moves did you make when the bond market begin to crack early in 1994?

I stopped buying bonds.

Had you known how much rates would shoot up, would you have done something more drastic?

Sure. But nobody ever knows. I have to run this fund on the assumption that we live in a stable economic and social environment. If I ever start to doubt that, the fund will look very different.

And right now, at any rate, you fear lower rates and early redemptions of bonds more than you fear higher interest rates?
I do. Higher rates mean I won't feel as good because the net asset value of the fund went down, but I'm going to get more income. Lower interest rates today would be a going-out-of-business event.

You mean you'd have nothing to buy?
In time, everything we own—every bond—would be gone, and a lot quicker than you think. Shareholders would be happier than all get-out, because they'd be looking at huge capital gains. But the show would be over for them.

They'd have to settle for 3% yields from Treasury bonds. . . .
If we get to that, I'm folding the fund. You cannot have a good reason for bonds to exist when you're down to yields that low.

The great irony is that if rates go to 2% or 3% the total returns are going to be stupendous and everybody in the world will be mindlessly pouring money into bonds.
I know. They probably will, and it will be a great time to take the money and invest in real estate.

Talking with Daniel Fuss you begin to see that buying and selling bonds is not such a mindless exercise, after all. Fuss has likened the bond market to a bowl of Jell-o, because everything has an effect—push it here and it juts out there. You could also compare bond investing to chess, because to know which way the Jell-o will bulge when punched by changing interest rates, you have to factor in a thousand sometimes-contradictory elements.

The Fuss method—buy below normal price, sell at normal price, diversify by type of bond, avoid early redemptions, keep your eye on income and don't be afraid of long maturities—has made Loomis Sayles Bond shareholders a fortune, as these calendar-year total returns attest:

	Loomis Sayles Bond	Average Corporate Bond Fund
1992	14.3%	7.1%
1993	22.2	9.7
1994	-4.1	-2.9
1995	32.0	15.8
1996 to November 1	8.1	2.8

When the long-maturities of its bonds should have hurt the fund seriously, in 1994 and again in 1996, the crosscurrents of all those different types of bonds held back the bleeding. So remember: Higher interest rates can be good for you.

Kenneth Heebner

T his man has made more money for investors the past 15 and 20 years than anyone else continuously running the same mutual fund. But just how Kenneth Heebner does it defies simple explanation or pat formulas. You can't pin labels on him because he's all over the place. The handsome, firm-featured Bostonian belongs to the old-fashioned school of stock picker who follows no technique that could be taught in a classroom, but who grabs ideas wherever they lie.

To the degree you can even describe the way Heebner goes about his business, it would be that he searches for a handful of stocks that he feels will surprise the rest of the investment world with their earnings, then bets the farm on his convictions. The result? CGM Capital Development, the fund (among five that he manages) that epitomizes his technique, returned an annualized 22% for the two decades ending in late 1996, versus 14.5% for Standard & Poor's 500-stock index. That may not seem like much of a lead, but across the span of 20 years it's the difference between having a $1,000 investment grow to $14,268 on the one hand, and $44,290 on the other. Alas, Cap Development is closed to new investors.

Heebner, who was born in 1940, exudes in person an enthusiasm for his job that you'd expect from a 20-year-old. But maybe you would whistle a happy tune, too, if you worked 45 floors above the street, with a spectacular view of Boston Harbor. That's where this first interview took place, in the summer of 1992.

KIPLINGER'S: You keep very concentrated portfolios in your two biggest funds—$1.8 billion invested in only 50 or so stocks. Does this reflect your investing style—or a lack of opportunities in other stocks?

HEEBNER: It reflects my style. I'm looking for unusual opportunities. And not many stocks stand out. When I find such stocks, I want to own them to the limit.

Aren't you taking big risks that way?

I do take big risks on occasion. And I've been burned. I got into Texas Air at $18 and rode it down to $6.50. What you want to do, obviously, is get rid of the ones that are hurting you and let the others run.

Your portfolio is eclectic: growth stocks, value stocks, huge companies, small companies—

I'm looking for a decisive advantage, wherever I find it. I want a company I think is great but the rest of the world has never heard of, or a company the rest of the world thinks is going broke. I want as big a discrepancy as possible between my view and the world's view. Since the world is pretty smart, it's very hard to have a vastly different opinion—and to be right.

So I don't care about size. I don't care about dividend yield. I don't care about the price-earnings ratio. I have no problem with a P/E of 25 if the earnings will go up enough.

Actually, today I have a tendency to be a low-P/E manager because that's my view of the market. You should be putting your money into value stocks. Two years ago was the time to have invested in profit growth.

So you're comfortable in either the growth or value camp?

I go anywhere I can make money. I have a bias toward stocks with strong earnings growth. You'll never see cyclical stocks grossly overpriced. Everybody knows a steel company and won't overvalue it. But you can get a freebie owning a growth stock—people get carried away.

The price goes to the heavens—

Yes. People overshoot. Right now, growth investing scares me. Everyone thinks it's the way to fast money. Everyone is comfortable with it. But I look for the growth stocks to go down more. I won't touch them. You don't wipe out years of excesses in three months.

Do you expect, then, that value will be the dominating theme for the next year or two?

Growth is going to get trashed. The Home Depots, Costco Wholesales and Blockbuster Entertainments will be crucified as their P/E ratios contract. Value stocks will perform relative to the overall market. And the overall market? I'm concerned when the average stock sells for 20 times earnings. People are paying too much for growth stocks. Ignorance is rampant in the stock market.

The fact that people are going from certificates of deposit to growth funds is a sign that there's ignorance in the marketplace, on a broad scale. What happens when these people start to experience capital depreciation? They're going to become upset and will never buy another stock. My dad was a building contractor. He came into the market in 1946 at a peak and bought four stocks. They went down and he never bought another.

What's your cash position?

Zero. I've raised big cash positions twice—in 1981, correctly, and in 1988, incorrectly. My appetite for doing it again is not great. I'm not good at timing markets.

Where do you get your ideas?

I look at huge numbers of companies all the time. I read all the material that comes from analysts at all the brokerages. What I'm seeking is a business whose earnings are going to be a surprise and therefore aren't already reflected in the stock's price. For instance, right now I have a huge position in Chemical Banking [since merged with Chase Manhattan]. My view of the banks is that in three or four years they will have fully recovered. They will have charged off their bad loans and won't be making many provisions for new write-offs. And I ask what Chemical Banking would earn if there were no charge-offs, or if it earned 1.1% on assets instead of a much lower level now. You come up with huge numbers—$6, $7, $8, $10 a share.

The stock is $36. [At the time of the merger with Chase in mid 1996, Chemical shares traded at about $60.] That's cheap. And it is a scenario others aren't focusing on.

You've also bought stocks of lots of smaller companies, such as Home Shopping Network in its infancy. Where do you come up with these ideas? Do they just walk in the door?

I don't do anything you can explain. I go to a lot of meetings between companies and analysts. I read brokerage reports religiously. I go to lunches several times a week. The factors I see that will produce earnings surprises are simply based on 25 years spent looking at companies.

One thing I do with companies that go up and down with the economic cycle is look at history. If Ford Motor earned the profit margin on cars today that it did in 1987, it would earn $12 to $15 a share. If Ford is going to earn $15 a share, it will be a $60 stock. Today it's at $45. That's pretty good, and in a declining market Ford would be a heck of an opportunity, and I'd buy. But you know, I don't see other people using historical ratios such as these to predict the profitability of companies.

How do you decide whether the price is right?

Remember, I'm looking for future earnings surprises. If a dramatic acceleration in earnings is not well known, I'm going to assume that the spurt isn't reflected in the present price of the stock. That's why I don't worry about P/E ratios and such.

I'm very fixated on what the crowd is doing. Everybody and his brother owns Home Depot, for instance. Every brokerage recommends it. There are no surprises to be had in that stock.

Isn't the same true of Philip Morris, one of your holdings?

True, everyone knows about Philip Morris. But their expectations of it aren't great—the P/E ratio is 12 times next year's earnings.

It is an arduous job managing $3.5 billion in 40 or 45 stocks?

Obviously you're very sensitive to every single company you own. They're all very important. If something goes wrong with one of them, it's going to cost me.

So are you always retesting the hypothesis on which you bought a stock?

Absolutely. Take Philip Morris. The key variables: Will the pricing of cigarettes hold? Will cigarette consumption in the U.S. continue to decline slowly? Will the Supreme Court say that warning labels protect PM against lawsuits?

If the court invalidates the protection of warning labels, won't you regret owning the stock?

Juries are not going to reward dead smokers. People don't like smokers—I don't care what the law says. Juries aren't going to say, "This guy smoked himself to death, so therefore his relatives deserve all this money," because the jurors once sat next to somebody at a party who blew smoke in their face. If the court goes against Philip Morris, it will trade down $2 a share, then go straight up from there. The price already assumes an adverse ruling. [The Supreme Court later ruled that tobacco companies could be held liable in some cases. Share prices fell only briefly.]

That's the sort of analysis I do—broad and simple, rather than narrow and complex.

But you don't fancy yourself to be a market timer?

No. Every time I'm bearish on the market, it keeps going up. So I just say I don't know what the market is going to do. A judgment I'm better able to make is that growth stocks are probably vulnerable, and in such cases I'm probably right. Over the years I've done better guessing the direction of groups of stocks than guessing the future of the overall market.

There are several themes in my portfolio now. Bombay Club, OnBanc and Collective Bancorp are the undiscovered stocks. With these I am investing in small-capitalization companies. Chemical Banking and Chase Manhattan are my contrarian stocks. With Philip Morris I function as a growth-stock investor with a contrarian thrust. How many people do you know who would say, "I think the tobacco business is one of the most exciting businesses in the world, and I'm privileged to be able to buy the shares of Philip Morris." That's what I say. I wish there were five more Philip Morrises.

After buying, how long will you wait for your ship to come in?
Every day I scan the portfolio and ask, "Given everything I'm looking at, can I make a lot of money from here on with what we own?" If a stock runs up and up, I'll sell. If something goes wrong with a company, I'll always sell. Right now I'm sitting on Green Tree Acceptance, and it's sitting there looking right back at me. It makes loans to buyers of mobile homes. That industry hit a 27-year low last year. But I expect Green Tree to earn $5 a share next year, and the stock is at $35. I've never had to wait two years for a stock to prove me right. It's more likely to be six months.

If you could own only five stocks for the next year, which ones would they be?
Let's see—Philip Morris, Telefónos de Mexico, Chemical Banking, Chase Manhattan and Syntex. Chase is a mediocre bank. But if you hold the net interest margin where it is now and just halve the loan-loss provision, it will earn $7 a share. The price now is $28. See? Simple. If it gets too complicated, I don't do it. [Chase stock had topped $60 at the time of the merger with Chemical in 1996.]

And if you could own just one stock for the next five years?
Easy. Philip Morris.

Heebner was remarkably prescient that afternoon—up to a point, at least. Yes, value stocks did have a long, long run, and CGM Capital Development sailed through 1992 with a return that was ten percentage points better than the S&P 500, and through 1993 with a seven-point lead. Meanwhile, a lot of Wall Street's favorite growth companies saw both their growth rates and share prices contract—Home Depot among them.

But it's the nature of a risk-taker like Heebner to walk off the cliff every so often, and he did just that in 1994, just as he had in 1988–'89 and 1983–'84. Or as he wryly puts it: "The record shows severe periodic underperformance." In the case of CGM Capital Development during 1994, it was a loss of 23%, which made it the *worst* long-term-growth fund for that year while also the best such fund for the past five.

Kiplinger's writer Manuel Schiffres and I revisited Heebner in Boston to ask what went wrong. "I always have overconcentration," he said. "In 1994 I put 60% of the portfolio into commodity cyclicals." In our original interview, he had said, "Everybody knows a steel company and won't overvalue it." Yet in early 1994, 25% of CGM Capital Development was invested in steel stocks. But that wasn't really inconsistent with his beliefs. Wall Street expected a soft economy and soft demand for steel, and Heebner anticipated the opposite scenario.

It didn't work his way. The sharp upward run in interest rates in 1994 took the steam out of the economic engine, and steel companies suffered accordingly. Heebner made no excuses for himself—admitting error seems easy. But almost casually he added: "I never make a point of this, because when you're wrong you're wrong, but had that strategy worked and the economy continued to grow, the steel stocks could have tripled and quadrupled, and CGM Capital Development, instead of being down 23%, could have doubled." In other words, there was a huge opportunity—except it didn't work. "I'm not always going to be right," said Heebner. "The important thing is, when I'm wrong I've got to recognize it, sell and move on, which I did." In 1995, Capital Development bet big on airlines, and the fund returned 41%—better than the S&P 500 and better than nine out of ten stock funds.

And Philip Morris, the stock he would own beyond all others?

Within months he didn't own a share. Heebner caught a whiff of what lay ahead—that the big tobacco company would decide to combat the inroads of cheap generic cigarettes by cutting prices, at the cost of short-term profits—and sold ahead of the news. Yes, love is fleeting.

A parting question: Any chance that Cap Development would reopen to new investors? Not a prayer. "I don't know how much money I can run," Heebner replied. "I started with $100 million, and now, all things together, I manage 50 times as much." In so doing, he said, he enlarged the universe of stocks in which he worked, and to some extent altered his style of management. But Heebner isn't willing to make such compromises again. "If you make a mis-judgment and take on too much," he said, "you risk mismanagement and the loss of your record and your reputation. I don't know why anyone would risk that."

Michael Hirsch

This book is all about how fund managers invest your money. But how should you invest your money in funds? Fund managers can't tell you much—their own money is typically wrapped up in their own funds. Michael Hirsch straddles this chasm. He manages the FundManager group—funds that invest in other funds, to the tune of almost $200 million. A self-described mutual fund junkie, Hirsch may know more about more funds than any other person on earth, and his 1991 book, *Mutual Fund Wealth Builder* (HarperBusiness), has become the bible of many fund investors. It stands to reason, then, that the methods Hirsch employs to evaluate funds are ones the rest of us ought to at least consider.

How I first met Hirsch tells you something about the man. He lectured on funds one evening at the Young Women's Hebrew Association in Manhattan, better known to New Yorkers as simply the 92nd Street Y. In the audience was Beatrice Shelley, who came up to Hirsch afterward and said she was among a cadre of Prodigy Interactive Service users who engaged in online discussions about funds. Mike said, "That's terrific! Invite them all to my office for the day." Bea sent out the word on Prodigy, and on the appointed day in the spring of 1994, a dozen of us came from as far away as Kansas City to meet a total stranger for lunch and to talk mutual funds. Two others called long-distance, from Denver and Los Angeles, to listen on the speakerphone.

Mike was a terrific host. We ate in the executive dining room of the Republic National Bank—at the time, his base of operations—and discussed investing for four hours. I didn't agree then with all of his opinions—I still don't—but I respected the man for the intensity of his beliefs, and for his willingness to listen to others. Early in 1995 I was back at Republic Bank, for this dialogue.

KIPLINGER'S: FundManager Aggressive Growth is packed

with long-term-growth funds. Is it fair to say that your watchword is "caution"?

HIRSCH: You should probably call it FundManager Less-Aggressive Growth fund. I have two qualifications for acquiring an aggressive fund. First, does the fund invest in non-mainstream names? If you look at its ten largest holdings and they're mainly non-S&P 500 stocks, it qualifies as far as I'm concerned. And second, is the manager really trying to beat the S&P 500 by a wide margin year to year?

Your investment methods in each of your funds are cautious almost to a fault. Does this reflect a fear that we're going to be hit by a terrible bear market, such as the one we had in 1973–'74?

No, although the funds obviously do well in huge downdrifts. But that's not what drives us. We are driven by the desire to be consistent. I have three criteria for putting a fund into a FundManager fund: consistent performance, consistent people and consistent investment philosophy or process. You can have an aggressive-growth fund that tries to hit doubles and triples. They don't all have to swing for home runs like Dreyfus Strategic Investing, which was down 11% in 1994, or American Heritage, which lost 35%.

In *Mutual Fund Wealth Builder*, you recommend that fund investors take the temperature of the stock and bond markets regularly, using fundamental indicators, and make all sorts of little adjustments. Isn't it asking a lot of people that they try to anticipate markets?

There will be times when doing nothing is best of all—last year, for example. Whichever way you turned would probably have been wrong. We made no adjustments on the bond side, and only a few on the stock side.

And you still got paid all that money. What a great job! In making adjustments, aren't you really timing the markets?

No. I'm talking about 5% adjustments, say, from aggressive growth to conservative growth—never as much as 25% or 50%.

Shouldn't most investors determine what asset allocations are best suited to them, buy the appropriate funds and then stick to their plan, rather than try to be their own portfolio managers and move things around according to how they feel about the market?

Exactly. Most people are best off with a fixed mix of funds that they adjust now and then to bring it back into balance.

And when one fund goes up more than the others, you sell the excess and buy more of those that didn't go up as much?

That's right—that is, if you're not of a mind to dump all your money into FundManager Managed Total Return fund, where I'll do it for you. The fixed allocation I would recommend would be a neutral one, which means you're not especially bullish or bearish.

None of your funds owns any international funds. Why not?

I have nothing against investing internationally if I can buy international stocks and bonds and not get involved in currency exchanges. The saying of currency traders is, "You trade foreign currencies; you don't invest in them." Yet Mr. Joe Mainstream—the unsophisticated Main Street U.S.A. investor—has been persuaded that he should make a five- or ten-year investment in an international fund, and therefore becomes an investor in foreign exchange as well as in foreign stocks.

Martin Wade, who manages T. Rowe Price International, has talked to us about his fund. "Martin," I said, "the day you start an international fund that hedges out all foreign exchange, I'll be your first investor."

So you would say that exposing yourself to currency risk is rank speculation?

Yes. But we do invest in global funds. They have the option to invest partly or totally in U.S. stocks if the dollar goes into a period of ascendancy, and the vast majority of them allow for currency hedging.

There has been no need to hedge for the past decade—the dollar's value has trended down the whole time.

Let's admit the truth: From the time the group of finance ministers met at the Plaza Hotel a decade ago [and agreed to push down the dollar's value versus other currencies], more than 50% of the reported gains of international funds has been attributable to foreign-exchange conversion and not to any fund-picking prowess. Not so long ago the Securities and Exchange Commission proposed a rule that would require funds to disclose the percentage of returns that came from currency conversion. The industry went ballistic and fought it.

I simply do not want to own currencies. The people who come to my funds are looking for risk-averse returns. I can't convince myself I give them that if I have a high exposure to an unhedged currency position. What if in the next ten years the dollar is in ascendancy? I'd wreck my shareholders.

Looking at the FundManager funds, their records are average to a bit below average. They also have high expense ratios, of roughly 1.7%. What keeps those ratios so high?

The asset sizes. Our funds are small—there's no getting around that fact. The loads we pay to buy some load funds are really not a factor because virtually all load funds now drop their loads for very big investors. The only ones that still charge us a sales fee are IDS Selective and Davis New York Venture.

You said earlier that you choose funds for the FundManager portfolios by performance, people and process. How do you judge performance?

Never use cumulative returns—they're the biggest trap of all. I look at year-by-year returns—for instance, for 1994, for 1993, and so on. I go back five years. Pension consultants make fortunes selling this theme to clients: Managers who provide consistent performance after five, ten or 15 years will far outrank managers who have a couple of spectacular years but a couple of dog years thrown in, too. If your fund simply stays in the 25th to 50th percentile among its peers, eventually it will show up among the top 10% long term. All it takes to achieve long-term success is slightly above-median returns.

How far back do you insist on above-average returns before buying a fund?

At a minimum, for each of the previous three years.

And if they later dip below the median in return, do you dump 'em?

Once they're in our fund portfolio, we can live with a year in the 55th percentile. After all, even tortoises slow down for a drink of water.

But you held on to Mutual Beacon even though it was in the bottom 10% for two years in a row. Why?

That's another part of the story. You see, Mike Price called to tell me in advance that his funds were going to underperform.

Funny, we must have been away from the phone when he called us . . .

Chuck Royce called me before Pennsylvania Mutual fund slipped.

Has anyone called lately with advance notice of a slump?

No. Lots of funds call me to announce they're about to soar—especially the hare funds that aren't on our list. They say we're going to miss a golden opportunity. But if you look at certain funds, there's almost a predictive quality about when they're going to hit the tank. You know Ken Heebner [CGM Capital Development and CGM Mutual] is going to fall flat every three and a half years, the Twentieth Century funds every four years.

But over time the CGM funds amass terrific records. Isn't there room in a portfolio for a "hare" fund like one of these?

Look in the mirror and ask yourself: Are you going to hold on to this hare when it is down 40%? If the answer is yes, then bless you, put it in your portfolio.

Have you ever taken a fund out of FundManager because it got too big?

Years ago I sold Evergreen fund for that reason, and more recently, Janus Venture. Venture's size was clearly a great hindrance. Jim Craig and a couple of analysts talked to regional brokers and did a bit of their own research and came up with a few small-company ideas. But you can't find that many little ideas to fill up a $1.5-billion fund. The only way Jim could invest all his cash was to contaminate the research process by broadening the guidelines that he invested by.

On that note, how big is too big for a small-company fund?

Every rule has its exception, but if you can invest only $2 million or $3 million per stock, then $200 million in assets is pretty big.

You write in your book never to invest in a new fund. Yet FundManager Growth bought Oakmark when that fund was in diapers. And its manager had never run a fund.

Yes, but we had invested with Harris Associates in Chicago all those years, starting when Ralph Wanger had Acorn fund there. And I have to tell you about Oakmark's manager, Bob Sanborn: I was overwhelmed with him. This kid is so excited, I could tell he couldn't help but be a success. I'd also seen his record managing private accounts.

That brings us to the "investment process." What do you mean by that?

The manager has to be able to define clearly for us his process of running the fund. We won't simply accept that it's a growth-and-income fund. What screens do you use? What parameters do you apply? Define your playing field for me. If I'm going to have ten funds inside FundManager Aggressive Growth, I have to be sure that each has a defined investment process that differs from the other nine.

Which raises a question: What's the optimum number of funds for an individual investor's portfolio? You max out at ten . . .

But I'm not capped there. My gut feeling is that after the "bombs" we've seen go off this past year we would probably want to own more.

For an individual, you'd want a small-cap growth fund, a small-cap value fund, big-cap growth, big-cap value and maybe medium-cap growth. You'd want at least one international or global fund if you're not as risk-averse as I am, and at a minimum one growth-and-income and one equity-income to offset one another. Then two fixed-income funds, so you don't have to spread the interest-rate risk around, and a money fund. That's 11 funds.

Given Hirsch's innate caution, the year 1995—a ripsnorter if there ever was one, rewarding risk-takers most of all—should have been a disappointment. Yet all three of his all-stock funds did respectably, and FundManager Growth & Income, the meekest of the bunch, did best of all, returning 35.4%, versus 37.5% for the S&P 500 and 28.1% for the typical growth-and-income fund. "The only thing I can surmise," Hirsch said, "is that with the bond market doing so well in 1995, a lot of our growth-and-income managers who own bonds did well in that arena." The single best fund in that portfolio was staid old Washington Mutual Investors, whose distinguishing feature is that every stock it owns must qualify for inclusion in a bank trust account according to Washington, D.C., law. It returned 41.2%—a terrific performance for a fund with $18 billion in assets.

Fund investors would benefit from knowing which funds were in Hirsch's three stock portfolios at the start of 1995 and 1996, and why he made changes.

FundManager Aggressive Growth

1995	1996
Brandywine	Brandywine
Davis New York Venture	Davis New York Venture
FPA Capital	FPA Capital
FPA Paramount	Guardian Park Avenue
Guardian Park Avenue	Harbor Capital Appreciation
Harbor Capital Appreciation	New Perspective
New Perspective	Royce Premier
Pioneer Three	SoGen International
Templeton Growth	Templeton Growth
Third Avenue Value	

"SoGen International went from the Growth to the Aggressive Growth fund because I wanted all the global funds, including Templeton Growth, in the most-aggressive portfolio. FPA Paramount went to the Growth fund because we felt that Bob Sams, who runs it, makes such use of out-of-favor industries and cash that he was acting more like a conservative growth investor than an aggressive one. I felt that Third Avenue Value and Mutual Beacon should be in the same portfolio, so it went to FundManager Growth, too. Pioneer Three was dropped because it had become too consistent a laggard." Royce Premier was added to represent small undervalued stocks.

I mentioned that Acorn had just reopened to new investors. Wouldn't it be a good proxy for smaller companies? "Well, we're not running back in," Hirsch replied. "The last time I sat with Ralph Wanger, before we sold it, I asked if he was increasing the size of his positions in each stock. 'Nope.' Well, with the asset size then at about $1 billion, I said, 'You're going to need to own quite a few stocks.' 'Yup.' I said, 'Ralph, you can't follow hundreds of stocks by yourself.' 'I don't; I have a team.' 'How often do you see their opinion on each holding?' 'Well, we grade each stock 1 to 10—one meaning buy and 10 meaning sell—and we review the 1-2-3 and 8-9-10 stocks, the strong buys and the strong sells.' I said to myself, here we go—that means the 4-5-6-7 stocks won't get looked at until they become 8-9-10 stocks. We decided at that point it was a dilution of Acorn's former approach and wanted out." [Wanger now uses a different methodology; see page 156.]

FundManager Growth

1995	1996
AMCAP	AMCAP
Clipper	Clipper
Dodge & Cox Stock	Dodge & Cox Stock
Fidelity	Fidelity
Gabelli Asset	FPA Paramount
MAS Equity	Gabelli Asset
Mutual Beacon	MAS Equity
Neuberger & Berman Guardian	Mutual Beacon
Oakmark	Neuberger & Berman Guardian
Putnam Vista	Oakmark
SoGen International	Third Avenue Value

As noted, SoGen International went to the aggressive fund, and FPA Paramount and Third Avenue Value came from the aggressive fund. "Putnam Vista we dropped because they brought in a new manager who invests too strictly by what his number-crunching tells him. Gabelli Asset is on our watch list and may be on the way out. Mario is spread too thin. It has always been my fear that he has his hand in too many pots." (For more on Gabelli, see page 11.)

FundManager Growth & Income

1995	1996
Affiliated	Affiliated
AIM Charter	AIM Charter
Fidelity Advisor Equity Income	Fidelity Advisor Equity-Income
Hotchkis & Wiley Equity Income	Hotchkis & Wiley Equity Income
Invesco Industrial Income	T. Rowe Price Equity-Income
T. Rowe Price Equity-Income	Vanguard Equity-Income
Vanguard Equity-Income	Vanguard Wellington
Vanguard Wellington	Washington Mutual Investors
Washington Mutual Investors	

Because this fund did the best of the three, it should come as little surprise that not much needed fixing. The only change was to drop Invesco Industrial Income, whose manager had been fired in

1994 for not following Invesco's rules on personal stock trades.

During 1995, I should add, Hirsch made some important changes in his operation. Republic Bank was going through a corporate reorganization that Hirsch felt left little place for his relatively small shop. So he is now affiliated with Freedom Capital, a subsidiary of John Hancock Financial Services. And his funds dropped their sales fees. "The maximum load allowed by law on a 'fund of funds' is only 1.5%," said Hirsch, "and that wasn't turning any brokers on. You may as well take the whole thing off, which I did. Now they are pure no-loads."

Considering that 1996 was the kind of year that rewarded shareholders of large companies, it should come as no surprise that the FundManager funds finished well behind the Dow Jones industrials. Indeed, they did only about half as well as the Dow and the S&P 500 index, which led to a final question: Do years like 1995 and 1996 make him wish his funds of funds were more risqué? "No," he replied. "In the end it will all even out. If you're too frisky on the upside, you're going to get clobbered someday, and I'm much more concerned about how I do on the downside than during the best times."

Brad Lewis

Y
ou won't even be tempted to invest in the manner of Brad Lewis—that is, unless you have a master's degree in computer science. His stock picker when we met in mid 1994 was a 90-megahertz personal computer. (It has since been upgraded.) I offer this interview for two reasons. One, no matter how he picks stocks, his Fidelity Disciplined Equity is one heck of a good fund, and one that *Kiplinger's* has cited as a possible substitute for an S&P 500 index fund. Two, I am impressed by his use of artificial intelligence to choose his portfolio. And Brad has only begun! After this interview he put a whole new system in place.

To give you an idea of how effective his methods are, Disciplined Equity was the only diversified U.S. stock fund at the start of 1995 that had outperformed the S&P 500 for each of the prior six years. Lewis could as easily be called program manager as portfolio manager, because his contribution is not picking stocks but writing the computer code that tells his PC how to do it.

Boston-based Lewis, born in 1955, is a "quantitative" investor. He's not particularly interested in the investment fundamentals of companies. He does want to know the factors that will propel a stock's price. A "quant" looks at massive amounts of data for clues about what is driving individual stocks, entire industries or the stock market itself.

The investment world is full of quants. What sets Lewis and a small band of other specialists apart is their use of computers to make sense of their data. Lewis programmed his PC to act as a "neural network." The best analogy to a neural net is the human brain. Normally, computer programs can sift through data to find a set of circumstances that you specify—for instance, stocks with earnings growth of 20% or more but with price-earnings ratios of 15 or less. A neural network doesn't need to be told what cause-and-effect relationships to look for. It discovers what moves a stock's price upward by learning those patterns from the data it processes, just as you might if you were in the mood to look at millions of pieces of information all night long.

Fidelity Disciplined Equity's assets are divided among industry groups to match the weightings of Standard & Poor's 500-stock index. But the fund is not limited to S&P 500 stocks, which is where the neural net earns its keep. Two smaller funds, Fidelity Stock Selector and Fidelity Small Cap, are also run by Lewis in the same manner and without the constraints of Disciplined Equity.

KIPLINGER'S: We keep imagining that you come to work each morning, unlock a black box and remove a single sheet of paper with exquisite handwriting that says: "Buy Upjohn and Pepsi. Sell Merck and Coke. Bring two virgins and one fatted calf." What really goes on?

LEWIS: It's three virgins, and the computer isn't black.

Let's start at the beginning. You don't have one computer program, but a bunch, right?

Correct. Just about every weekend the neural-network program grinds away from Friday night until Monday morning. What it produces is the expected return over the next nine months of 2,800 stocks.

To come up with those expected returns, what is the program looking at?

The returns will be affected by many variables that people know—things like the stocks' price-earnings ratio the next 12 months, the leverage, the price-to-book ratio, insider buys and sells, and, on a larger level, what the yield curve looks like and how the business cycle is proceeding and affecting different companies.

And your program takes this raw data and spits out which stocks will do best and worst?

You can't just take the industrial-production statistics, for example, and dump them into a neural network—they're useless that way. The trick is to take this data and other data from many different sources and transform it. For instance, you first calculate rates of change in industrial production, and you decide whether six-month or 12-month rates of change are more predictive of the future. I spend probably 35% of my time writing computer code that implements ideas like this for using the data.

What will the neural network be looking for—sets of circumstances that cause a stock's price to rise?

Yes. Let's say that General Electric is a buy when the yield curve is accelerating upward. This isn't a pattern that will jump out at you. You've got to have a methodology to find that pattern. And the hypothesis is that the factors that affected GE's stock price the past ten years will probably persist for the next year or two. On the other hand, look at IBM. The things that moved its stock in 1958 don't apply now—it's an entirely different company. That's one of the things a quant has to deal with—how far back to reach for historical data to put into neural networks.

And neural nets "learn" from this data?

Yes. I used to use multiple regressions, which keep testing different combinations. A regression will give you a formula that's the best way to weigh the different factors you feed into it. A neural net is essentially the same thing, but it will learn to find nonlinear patterns, which are pretty important.

What's a nonlinear pattern?

One that's not a straight line. Assume that the price-to-book-value ratio of a stock is the function of its return on earnings. If the ROE goes up, so will the price-to-book ratio. But if you get an ROE of 25%, the price-to-book really starts to explode on you. That's a nonlinear relationship. The neural net learns very fast how a lot of variables combine to affect a stock's price.

What does the data from the neural net look like when it finishes its work?

It's just a data file, unintelligible to normal human beings.

But once you translate it, does it tell you what to sell and what to buy, and the number of shares to sell and buy?

Oh, yes. Absolutely. That's another step—the optimizer. The neural net that runs all weekend generates the forecasts for 2,800 stocks. The optimizer takes those forecasts, factors in the liquidity of those stocks and the industries each is in, and gives me the optimum portfolio. The whole goal of Disciplined Equity is to beat the S&P 500 every single year. I've got to manage my industry risk carefully. If I let the computer run amok, it would pick 50 tiny small-company stocks.

So you build constraints into the optimizer?

Exactly. I say, "Maximize the portfolio's expected return, subject to these conditions." Obviously, the big constraint is liquidity. I generally don't like to own more than one day's average trading volume of a stock. If I've got a stock headed for trouble, and I own ten days' trading volume, it might take me 40 days to get out of that stock.

And the optimizer gives you a buy/sell list?

Not quite. There's one final step: a third program that reconciles the optimum portfolio with what I currently hold. For instance, the optimizer might say I should own 100,000 shares of IBM. The third program will know I own 80,000 and tells me to buy another 20,000. Another example: Expected return is expressed as the alpha. Say I own United Technologies, and its alpha is 0.40, and that of Thiokol, also in the aerospace business, is 0.41. Now a stupid optimizer would say Thiokol has a higher expected return than UTX, so sell UTX and buy Thiokol. But the difference in their alphas could be no more than a rounding error. So I do things that prevent the system from making such a switch.

Your neural network doesn't actually forecast the direction of the stock market, does it?

No. That's another program! My advanced study project at Wharton [School of Finance] was an econometric market-forecasting model. I've kept it pretty current.

So you do forecast the future of the S&P 500?

I try to, and I adjust the aggressiveness of Disciplined Equity and Stock Selector accordingly. I'm not going to bet my career on a market-forecasting model. But at the margins I will take the beta of the portfolios up or down based on its forecasts.

Do you know why your computer says to buy or sell a stock? Can you isolate the factors?

No. I don't care. Obviously, I want the stock to go up after I buy it. I don't see a big need to know why. Five years ago I felt differently. Today I know this stuff works in most environments.

So you don't apply your own subjective judgment once the computer hands you its list of buys and sells?

Even less now than before. When I first started this, I did more second-guessing of the program. Usually I was wrong.

What stands out in your mind as your worst call against the program?

Probably buying a few airline stocks when the black box said not to. I was an airline analyst once. You should never buy airline stocks—that's a good rule to live by.

Suppose you go to a conference and hear something about a company that really whets your appetite. Will you buy that stock even if your computer says not to?

Yes, I will, if I know in advance that a company is going to report a quarter that's better than expectations. But that doesn't happen very often.

What's your worst nightmare running Disciplined Equity?

A real narrow market that persists for three or four years, without really going up or down. Also, when themes rule the market, I'm in trouble. When Hillary attacked all my health care stocks in 1993, it was not a pleasant experience. Then last October and November we had the information-superhighway-in-the-home nonsense, involving stocks I'd never own because they traded at 30 times earnings. But then those stocks went to 40 times earnings. That was a tough time, too.

Is it the stock market that you take pride in beating, or Vanguard Index Trust 500 fund?

That's a sore point. It drives me nuts to see $8 billion in that thing now. My fund has beaten it every single year.

There is a fair amount of competition between Fidelity and Vanguard, isn't there?

Yes, that's true. And there should be. It's good for investors.

You've been quoted as saying your own IRA money is in Stock Selector fund . . .

No. It's in Small Cap fund. That's an aggressive-growth portfolio.

Do you program Small Cap any differently than you do Disciplined Equity?

Just the optimizer. The same analysis goes into both. Disciplined Equity can choose among 2,800 stocks. Small Cap can choose among 1,900 of those same 2,800 stocks—the others being large companies. If small-cap stocks look awful, I may tweak the optimizer for Small Cap to include more of the stocks Disciplined Equity might buy.

Do shareholders of Disciplined Equity tend to be individuals or institutions?

Individuals. The 401(k) business is picking up.

**The reason we ask is that it is not easy to understand how
you run this fund . . .**

That's a problem!

**Wouldn't big pension funds be more comfortable with your
methods than ordinary investors?**

You're exactly right—pension plans are better for marketing this
fund. But I don't have a heck of a lot of interest in that. I'd have to
justify myself to all those pension-plan consultants. I would rather
stick a sharp pencil in my eye than do that. But the 401(k) money is
just great.

Brad Lewis, one of the nicest men you'll ever meet, is also the
personification of computer geek. To say that words pour from his
mouth hardly describes the speed with which they run together—
half of them a mixture of computer and Wall Street jargon, to which
Brad is oblivious. If you had trouble grappling with this printed
dialogue, you should have been there at the time.

Anyway, in October of 1995 we were back in Lewis's office, to ask
about his new brain—new software that qualifies as true artificial
intelligence. He'd read a technical paper on AI that led him to believe
he could achieve better stock-selection results. So Brad began
churning out C-language computer code and some months later had
a new brain that "kicked the neural net's butt" in terms of stock
selection. I asked him to explain the difference between his old brain
and the new one. "The neural network wasn't considered artificial
intelligence," he explained. "AI finds nonlinear relationships better.
Take two stocks: Microsoft and Duke Power. If each stock has its
earnings estimate cut by 5%, whose stock will take the biggest
percentage loss? Microsoft [because people invest in it for earnings
growth]. That's nonlinear. Or compare Micron Technology with
Duke Power. If they each cut their dividend a little, which would be
hurt most? Duke Power [because people invest in Duke for its
dividend]. That's nonlinear, too."

January of 1995—the last month for the neural network—had been one of the worst ever for Disciplined Equity. Its total return for the month trailed that of the S&P 500 by four percentage points. But the new artificial intelligence software had made up the difference in what would normally be a terrible investment climate for this fund— one driven by a theme, namely technology. Brad figured he'd end the year ahead of the S&P 500, again.

Instead, Disciplined Equity's new brain seemed to suffer memory lapse. In November of 1995, and again in December, the fund trailed the S&P 500 by about three percentage points. For the year of 1995, the fund trailed by more than eight percentage points. In January of 1996, the shortfall was another two percentage points.

In February, the fund beat the S&P 500, by about a percentage point. Thereafter, the road for Disciplined Equity got rough again, and by early December it trailed the S&P by eight percentage points again—the second annual disappointment by a fund that isn't supposed to disappoint its investors.

Was artificial intelligence being humbled? Quite possibly. Maybe you cannot train even the fastest computers to find every relationship between economic numbers or market activity and the price of a stock. Or maybe, despite all our efforts to explain the behavior of the stock market, it sometimes acts without reason—or rather, against all reason.

Be Your Own Manager

I said at the beginning of this book that one of the major reasons for these mutual fund managers' success is that they formulate a strategy and stick with it, tweaking it as necessary. You've read the interviews, and you've seen for yourself. Bottom line: They've learned to do something well.

That's another way of saying, get in a groove. The managers of these mutual funds are all in a groove. They've learned to invest one way, and they do it well. It's as simple as that—and as hard as that.

I will be frank: As a stock picker I was unable to adopt a style or method, learn it and stick to it. I'd buy one stock for one reason, another for another, and so on, soon forgetting why I had bought them in the first place. I sold these stocks in just as undisciplined a fashion. I had no anchor, and lacking that, the returns I enjoyed weren't very impressive. That's why I now invest primarily in mutual funds. True, I still have to pick the funds, but it's far easier to do that wisely than to choose individual stocks.

You can do better investing in stocks than I did. *How to Pick Stocks* has presented a feast of ideas—a banquet of more than two dozen investment methods laid out for you to devour. Some are utterly unique, others are variations on the same theme. One or more of these are likely to appeal to you. You can apply them in your own stockpicking, or like me, you may choose to invest in the fund itself or one like it, taking advantage of the managers' experience. In a moment, I'll show you how.

Critical Elements of Your Investment Plan

But before you start, let's touch on a few basic investing do's and don'ts, which even old hands at investing should reconsider occasionally.

Know Why You're Investing

I know people who invest for the thrill of it. They thrive on the risks, the intellectual challenge and all that. But even they undoubtedly began, on square one, for some rational reason, such as accumulating enough wealth at one end of life to permit them to throttle back in comfort at the other end. I suggest you do the same. Before you buy those 100 shares of Microsoft or open that account at Vanguard Group, set a goal. Make it one worthy of your time and capital. Who wants to invest "for a comfortable retirement"? That's as inspiring as yogurt. But try this: to buy that house you saw in Carefree, Arizona, overlooking the golf course on one side and the cactus-splattered Maricopa mountains on the other, and to produce $4,000 a month in income on top of that. Whatever your goal, put a price beside it, and beside that, the time you've got to accumulate this capital.

Keep Risk on a Leash

You can define risk many ways. For the sake of simplicity, let's say it is *the chance that you won't earn from your investing the return that you should rationally expect*. What does that mean? Suppose you have a 15-year time frame and are investing in stocks of established companies with steady growth in earnings, year after year. Essentially, these are companies included in Standard & Poor's 500-stock index. Thanks to the folks at Ibbotson Associates, which does investment research, we know that this index over the past 70-odd years has returned 10% to 11% on an annualized basis—15% the past

15 years. (These numbers assume you have reinvested dividends in more shares of the same stocks.) Go ahead, be ambitious, set a goal of earning 15% per year from your stock picking. Your risk, therefore, is that you won't have achieved a 15% rate of return at the end of 15 years.

There is, of course, a relationship between risk and reward: The greater the reward you seek (and 15% per year *is* a generous reward), the more risk you must take. Or stated another way, the more risk you take, the more reward you should expect.

How can you keep risk under some sort of control? Here are the two best ways, plus some advice specifically for mutual fund investors:

Give Yourself Time.

I said that the S&P 500 returned 15% over the past 15 years, through 1996. But in no single year did the index actually return 15%. Rather, the returns varied quite widely, from a low of –7% in 1977 to a high of 38% in 1995. Those deviations above and below the long-term rate of return we call *volatility.* The more volatile your investment, the greater the *short-term risk* that you won't achieve your expected return, because from year to year markets are erratic and unpredictable. But volatility may not be bad for you over the long haul, considering that volatility works in your favor in rising markets and that stocks rise in price more than they fall. Moreover, with the passage of time your annualized rate of return becomes less erratic as one year's results are added to those of earlier years.

So the greater the rate of return you expect, the more time you should allow. Otherwise, your risk of not achieving it is too great. Achieving a 15% return across 15 years by investing in those established growth companies, while ambitious, is not unreasonable. Doing so in five years is. In five years you might *lose* money in this investment plan, particularly if you are building up a basket of growth stocks, starting with one and adding others as you can. If your time to invest is five years, you would be better off owning bonds—or better yet, a mutual fund that invests in less-volatile stocks as well as bonds.

Cast a Wide Net.

In a mutual fund, at least you get diversification. In the above example, you get diversification between asset classes—stocks and bonds. And in any fund, you get a lot of diversification within a type of assets—a lot of stocks or a lot of bonds.

Diversification does the same thing as time to hold down risk: It reduces the odds that one stock will be torpedoed by events and sink your whole investment plan. Owning shares in five established companies with steady earnings growth is therefore less risky than owning one, and owning ten less risky than owning five. (By averaging out the highs and lows of all these separate stocks, diversifying also reduces the likelihood that you will earn a 20% rate of return over 15 years, but that's the trade-off of reducing risk, and one that a wise investor will cheerfully accept.)

Put This Book to Use

You've read the profiles and, I hope, enjoyed engaging in some financial voyeurism. You've digested my admonitions. Now what? This section will help you put your new insights to use in one of three ways, described in order of the increasing amounts of time and knowledge, and the decreasing expense, they require.

Hire a Broker

If you have no desire to develop your portfolio of stocks on your own, you can use a full-service broker to help you. Use the profiles to identify your objectives and preferred style of investing. Then, lay out the guidelines you've come up with for your broker. Let him or her do the research and come to you with appropriate recommendations. The strategy you define will limit how often the broker interrupts your day with hot tips—and how much you'll pay in commissions—by eliminating impulsive trades.

Develop a Portfolio of Mutual Funds

Mutual funds offer the advantages of expert portfolio

management, convenient trades and shareholder service, and instant diversification. You can avoid sales commissions or high expense ratios by choosing no-load mutual funds. All you have to do is choose your funds and monitor them over time.

That's *funds,* plural. One probably won't be enough. Even though you'll get the advantage of diversification within any one fund, the fund manager's choices will be constrained by the fund's style—whether it focuses on big companies, small companies, fast-growing businesses, or those that are undervalued, or divides its assets between U.S. and non-U.S. stocks. Because different styles do better at different times, you ought to select a portfolio of funds that covers the bases, so that on average, over time, you get a decent return. Each fund can also be categorized by the degree of risk it accepts, from most aggressive to most conservative, in pursuit of the best possible return. Your portfolio should produce the return you want for the amount of risk you can afford given the time you have. For example:

- **If you're saving for your retirement,** you'll probably want a long-term investment plan—for a time horizon of, say, at least ten years—that's aimed at achieving maximum capital growth. You'll have a maximum tolerance for short-term volatility.

- **If your goal is college for the kids,** you'll want a less frisky portfolio with a seven-to-ten-year time horizon. You're looking for a portfolio that will give you a good return, but you haven't got as much time to recoup a major loss, so this one will be more conservative. For example, you might be looking at investing about 80% of your money in stock funds and the rest in a relatively aggressive bond fund.

- **A new home** within four to six years calls for a conservative, short-term plan. You might divide your investment evenly between stock funds located on the lower range of the volatility ladder and bond funds.

You can use many of the steps that you would otherwise use to pick individual stocks, outlined in the next section, to select your funds.

Pick Stocks Yourself

Chances are you read this book because you *do* want to do it yourself. Go back and reconsider the investing strategy (or strategies) that really appealed to you and follow the steps described below to learn all you can about how the fund manager whose style you like makes investment decisions. Then, because you're doing the research and selecting the stocks yourself, you can use a discount broker to make your trades.

- Select a mutual fund whose investment methods are compatible with your objectives and time frame.

- Call the fund and ask for recent shareholder reports.

- Read what the manager says in those reports.

- Think through what this manager is doing.

- Study what the fund invests in, and see if you can relate each holding to the manager's method.

- Visit your library and find out what *Morningstar Mutual Funds* or *Value Line Mutual Fund Survey* says about this manager's way of investing.

- Think of how you can adapt it to make it your own investing blueprint.

Because you'll have less access to the research that's available to fund managers, your method for picking stocks will probably be a simplification of what the professional investor does. That's okay, so long as it makes sense to you and is consistent with itself. If you're really serious about this, call the fund and ask to speak to the manager about your variation on his or her method. Most of these people will find the time to talk to you (particularly if you are an investor in the fund). After all, they love what they're doing. This is their life.

A "Shelby Davis Plan" for do-it-yourselfers

All this needn't be complicated, either. Let me give you an

example. I've always admired the record of Shelby Davis at Davis New York Venture fund (and now at Selected American Shares fund as well). I was eager to do an "Insider Interview" with him, and I wasn't disappointed with its outcome. Broken down to its simplest elements, the Davis method is to identify well run companies with excellent prospects for long-term earnings growth, wait patiently for those companies to sink into temporary disfavor, buy shares during that weak spell and then hold on nigh to forever.

Now, is that hard? Well, in fact, it is. Shelby Davis, his son and co-manager Chris, and however many analysts they employ at their beck and call go to enormous lengths to identify those "well run companies with excellent prospects for long-term earnings growth." Shelby roams the U.S. regularly to meet the CEOs and other executives of companies he thinks may fit his mold, and Chris is always on the phone doing the same thing.

But it's not unreasonable to expect that you could cuddle up with *Value Line Investment Survey* and come up with a lengthy list of companies that fit that mold. They would conceivably include many companies that are in the portfolios of the two Davis-run funds—in particular, consumer-goods companies (Coca-Cola, Gannett, Gillette, Johnson & Johnson, Seagram, [Chicago] Tribune Co.) and financial-service companies (American Express, Chubb, Equitable, Travelers Group, Wells Fargo).

Personally, I like those consumer companies. They're big, and as Donald Yacktman, of Yacktman fund, likes to say, it's hard to kill a big company. They sell many things, making them even more invulnerable to fickle winds of change. Their businesses don't depend a lot on the state of the economy, so they'll do okay even in a serious business recession. And by and large, their earnings and their dividends go up year after year—just look at their stock-price charts on the pages of *Value Line* and admire their steady upward progress over time. Yum.

So to get in this groove, you now draw up a list of 30 to 40 prospects that a Shelby Davis–type investor would love. Call their headquarters (phone numbers are listed in *Value Line*) and ask for copies of shareholder reports for the past several years. Also obtain prospectuses of their dividend-reinvestment plans (DRIPs)—virtually all big companies have them now. Which ones involve the lowest fees to reinvest dividends or to buy additional shares (once you own at least one share) directly from the company? If you are the client of a full-service brokerage, ask for its research reports on these same stocks. Read what *Value Line* has to say about them.

Next, rank these companies in the order that you'd like to own them, giving most weight to your judgment of their long-term prospects and to diversification among different industries, and less weight to the attractiveness of the dividend-reinvestment plans. Among those on the top half of your list, are any in trouble— in Wall Street's doghouse? Bad things are always happening to good companies, and that's when you want to buy them.

Go to a broker and buy your first shares in at least a handful of stocks at the top of your list of companies that the rest of the investing world is *least* wild about—even one share each is okay. Once the shares are registered in your name, sign up for the DRIPs. At most this whole process will cost you $1,000. Then each month invest a set amount via the DRIP plans in additional shares of one or more of the stocks, favoring any that are in disfavor at that moment on Wall Street. (This gives you the added advantage of dollar-cost averaging, which, over the long run, lets you purchase more shares at low prices than you do at high prices.) Or expand your portfolio by adding new names if, say, a Gillette or a Coca-Cola takes a hit because its earnings rose only 12% in the latest three months instead of 13%.

Congratulations. You've used Shelby Davis's methods to launch your own investment plan. Keep on top of what is happening to companies tucked inside this little mutual fund you've just created. (My fantasy is that you'll see Shelby Davis quoted in *Kiplinger's Personal Finance Magazine* on the attractiveness of Cola-Cola just as Coke runs temporarily afoul of the barons of Wall Street and comes into buying range.) Don't be quick to sell or second-guess your decisions. And for goodness' sake, read the next section of this chapter.

If You Go With Mutual Funds

The interviews in this book will get you started thinking about which funds you'll want, but you might also want to take a look at the following resources. You can also use these to help track the progress of the funds you choose.

- **"Best Funds for Your Goals,"** an annual cover story of *Kiplinger's Personal Finance Magazine* (March), which offers suggested fund portfolios for investors with short-, medium- and long-term goals.

- **Our magazine's annual mutual fund roundup** (September), with performance rankings, volatility ranks, and masses of other data for more than 2,000 funds.

- *Kiplinger's Mutual Funds,* a newsstand publication (available each February) that provides fund recommendations and plenty of guidance on choosing funds.

And if you are really starting from scratch and want more advice on such basic issues as whether to do it yourself or hire a broker and whether to invest in load or no-load mutual funds, take a look at *Kiplinger's Invest Your Way to Wealth,* by Theodore Miller. It covers those questions and more, with whole chapters dedicated to how to use stocks and mutual funds.

Don't Be Distracted

Once you've done all this, what could possibly go wrong? Plenty! You open the newest issue of *Kiplinger's* and see that Hotdog Supercharged Small-Company Growth fund has just doubled its shareholders' money the past year. Holy cow. You've been buying these boring old razor-blade and cola companies when the *real* money is being made in the boutique stocks of companies that

didn't exist two years ago. You'd better get on that quick! Before
you know it your investment plan is in tatters. So, I'll wager, will be
your recent results.

You've just been distracted. Distractions come from the devil's
workshop, and are designed to make you doubt the wisdom of your
ongoing investments. They appear in front of the most successful
investors, beckoning them off the path they have established.

Distractions are in the voice of your broker Jack, who just heard
the Merrill Lynch semiconductor analyst on the squawk box say
that the book-to-bill ratios of the companies he follows are up
sharply, and that these stocks are therefore due for some big moves
on heavy volume. Maybe they are. But just because Jack and his
analyst are convinced there is money to be made, and soon, doesn't
mean you should do anything, unless it would fit like the piece of a
jigsaw puzzle into the investment tableau you have constructed.

Distractions are on the pages of *Barron's,* when a fund manager
you much admire makes the persuasive case for three small
companies whose earnings are doubling each year. No razor-blade
companies here, for sure.

Distractions are on the nightly news, whose anchorman reports
that the unemployment rate is rising, industrial production is
slipping and the Dow Jones industrial average just went down,
again—and then pauses ever so briefly with that serious, ironic look
on his handsome face. Tom *does* seem worried. Should you back off
and sell some shares?

Distractions abound in your favorite online investing discussion
forum, as excited folks swap tips on which stocks to buy tomorrow
morning and sell tomorrow afternoon.

Ignore all this. Ignore everything about investing that doesn't
have to do with your own investment plan. Pay attention to your
plan. Get it right. Keep it right. To heck with everything else. This
is how all of the subjects of this book conduct their business lives,
and this is what you must do, too, or else. Or else you'll be buying
things without knowing why, and therefore selling them without
knowing why. You'll be like a ship lost at sea.

Time and again in these interviews, remember, the subject went back to distractions:

- **James Craig of Janus fund:** "What generally happens to me if I break my discipline is that I don't know when to sell. It's just like buying off a hot tip from a broker. If I don't know why I own it, then I have absolutely no idea what I'm doing. I might just as well be speculating."

- **Shelby Davis: "**I try to focus on what is knowable and important rather than what's unknowable and important. What's unknowable and important is the market's next direction."

- **John Neff of Vanguard Windsor:** "You've got to have some sort of systematic approach or you won't know where you are."

- **Michael Price of Mutual Shares:** "I'm not trading stocks based on what I think will happen to the economy or based on my guess of the future of interest rates. I buy stocks only when they're available at the right price."

A few of these people alluded to the worst distraction of all. That's when even the family dog thinks you're dumb. You do all the right things and nothing happens. Your stocks sit still when the market goes up or your stocks go down when the market sits still. This has happened to all of the people interviewed in this book. How they've dealt with adversity—be it their own poor stock selection or a market that is temporarily punishing their sorts of stocks— sometimes defines their whole investment philosophy:

- **Neff:** "When stocks go down we're sometimes stupid enough to buy more. That's what we've always done. We do not listen to the marketplace. The only thing worse than being wrong is being whipsawed—you know, caving in at exactly the wrong moment and duplicating on the other side the losses you just suffered."

- **Price:** "I would come to work in 1990 and see letters on my desk every day. 'What kind of idiot are you, Mr. Price?' These were people who bought the fund in 1988 and early '89. . . . Then our shareholders lost 5% in the last half of '89 and another 9% in 1990. Now they were saying, 'Wait a minute! I thought this was a good fund.'. . . What could I tell them? I'm not changing what I do. I did in 1989 through 1991 exactly what I did in 1985 and '80 and '87 and today."

- **Donald Yacktman of Yacktman fund:** "There's a narrow difference between being stubborn and being determined. If you're right—and I was, ultimately—you're determined."

Now, you've seen how 27 of America's best mutual fund managers do their jobs. I think you'll agree with me that there's a lot for all of us to learn within these pages about the art of investing. My hope for you is that you can put this book down with the confidence that you, too, can be an intelligent investor, and that your dog will always think you're smart.

Investment Terms You Should Know

Arbitrage. An attempt to profit from price differentials. It may be the momentary difference in price of the same security on different markets or of different securities whose values are linked. Investors also arbitrage the difference between the current price of a stock and that which will be paid if a purchase of the issuing company is completed.

Back-end load. A commission charged when shares of a fund are sold. Often this fee declines or ends after a fixed number of years. See *front-end load.*

Bearish. A bear is someone who thinks the market will go down. To be bearish is the opposite of *bullish.*

Bid/asked. Bid is the price a buyer is willing to pay for a security; asked is the price the seller will take. The difference, called the *spread,* is kept by the broker.

Blue chip. In general, a company that is well known, has a long history of profits and dividends, and is widely owned by investors.

Bond. An interest-bearing debt security that obligates its issuer to pay interest for a set period of time and then to repay the face value of the bond upon maturity.

Bond rating. The judgment by a rating agency of a borrower's ability to pay interest and repay principal upon maturity. The best-known raters are Standard & Poor's Corp. and Moody's Investor's Service, both of which use similar letter grades for their ratings.

Book value. The net worth of a company, determined by subtracting its liabilities from its assets. Book value per share, once a notable yardstick of a company's relative value, has come into disuse because of restructurings and write-offs of assets.

Bullish. A bull is someone who thinks the market will go up. To be bullish is the opposite of *bearish*.

Capital gain or loss. The difference between the price at which an investment is bought and that at which it is sold.

Closed-end mutual fund. A pooled investment fund that issues a fixed number of shares, and then no more. Those shares thereafter trade like shares of stock on a stock exchange or over the counter, at prices determined by supply and demand, at either a discount or premium to net asset value.

Common stock. A share of ownership in a corporation that entitles its holders to the rewards if the business succeeds. In the event of failure, or bankruptcy, common stockholders' claims on assets of the corporation are inferior to those of bondholders.

Contrarian. An investor who thinks and acts in opposition to the common wisdom. When the majority of investors are bullish about a stock, an industry or the entire stock market, a contrarian is bearish, and vice versa.

Convertible bond. A bond that can be exchanged for a fixed number of shares of a company's common stock at a fixed price. The appeal of a convertible is that a holder can benefit if the price of the stock soars.

Derivative. A security whose value depends on changes in the value of another security. Commonly known derivatives would include put and call options and futures contracts. Less well known are structure derivatives, such as inverse floaters and interest-only or principal-only securities.

Dividend. A share of a company's earnings paid out to shareholders, or the total dividends earned by a mutual fund portfolio and passed on to shareholders of the fund.

Dividend-reinvestment plan. Also called a DRIP, this is a program under which a company automatically reinvests a shareholder's cash dividend in additional shares of common stock, usually without a brokerage commission. Many DRIP plans also allow participants to buy additional shares directly from the company.

Duration. A measure of the sensitivity of the portfolio of a bond mutual fund to a one-percentage-point change in interest rates. A fund with a duration of six years, therefore, is liable to lose 6% of its value if the interest rate on similar bonds rises by one percentage point—or to rise by 6% if the rate on similar bonds falls by one percentage point.

Earnings per share. A company's profits after taxes, bond interest and preferred-stock payments have been subtracted, divided by the number of shares of common stock outstanding.

Expense ratio. The percentage of a mutual fund's total assets that shareholders pay annually for operating expenses and management fees. The expense ratio does not include a *front-end load* or *back-end load* but does include the *12b-1 fee*, if any.

Front-end load. The commission charged on the purchase of shares of a mutual fund. See *back-end load*.

Fundamental analysis. Study of the balance sheet, earnings, history, management, products and other elements of a company in an effort to estimate its future earnings and share price.

Growth investor. Someone who seeks the stocks of companies with rapidly growing profits.

Initial public offering. A company's first public offering of stock. Also called an IPO.

Junk bond. A high-risk, high-yield bond rated BB or lower by Standard & Poor's or Ba or lower by Moody's. Their issuers are financially weak or little-known companies, and they carry noticeably higher yields than investment-grade corporate bonds.

Liquidity. The ability to quickly convert an investment portfolio to cash without suffering a noticeable loss in value. Stocks and bonds of large, widely traded companies are considered liquid. Real estate is illiquid.

Load. The sales commission charged at the time of purchase or redemption of a mutual fund. See *front-end load* and *back-end load*.

Mutual fund. A pooled investment in stocks, bonds or money-market instruments that is professionally managed and divided into shares, whose value will hinge on that of the underlying investments.

Open-end mutual fund. A *mutual fund* that invests in stocks, bonds or money-market instruments and will continuously sell and redeem shares at net asset value.

Par. For bonds, the face value when issued. Because the face value of a bond can differ, prices quoted in newspapers are a percentage of the face, or par, value.

Preferred stock. A class of stock that pays a specified dividend when it is issued. Preferreds generally pay less income than the *bond* of the issuing company but more income than its *common stock*. Preferred stocks stand to lose less in poor stock-market periods, but gain less in a *bullish* climate, than a company's common stock.

Price-earnings ratio. The price of a stock divided by its earnings per share. Newspapers report the P/E ratio based on the past 12 months of earnings. But investors tend to base decisions on predicted earnings, so it is important to know the time period on which a P/E ratio is quoted. In any event, it is a measure of fundamental value because it indicates how much investors are willing to pay for a dollar of earnings.

Price-sales ratio. A stock's price divided by sales per share. This is a measure, much like the *price-earnings ratio*, that is favored by some investors as a sign of a stock's relative value. Some investors favor the P/S ratio because the P/E ratio is affected by special charges and earnings, whereas actual revenue is less susceptible to manipulation.

Prospectus. For mutual fund investors, the document that divulges financial information and sets forth the investment criteria, risk factors, management fees and other expenses, and other information necessary for an informed decision.

Return on equity. A measure of investment results, in which you divide shareholder equity—that is, the total value of common and preferred stock—into a company's net income after taxes.

Short selling. The reverse of the normal buying and selling of a stock. A short seller borrows shares of a stock from a broker and sells those shares in anticipation of buying an equal number of shares at a later date at a lower price. The profit is the difference between the sale and purchase prices. A short seller can realize a 100% profit only if the shares become worthless. But if the price of the stock increases, there is no limit to the loss. Repurchasing shares "covers" the short sale.

Sinking fund. Money set aside to be used exclusively to redeem a bond or preferred-stock issue and thus assure investors that the company will be able to meet its obligation to repay its debt.

Spread. The difference between the *bid* and *asked* prices for a security. This is a form of broker markup, and is in addition to any commission that may be charged.

Standard deviation. A measure of an investment's volatility. It expresses the degree to which the investment's price tends to vary, up or down, from its average price.

Technical analysis. An approach to markets that forecasts future results by looking at past price trends, trading volume and other stock-market statistics.

Total return. A measure of investment performance that adds to price changes the results of reinvesting capital gains and income that were produced during the period being measured.

12b-1 fee. An extra fee charged by some mutual funds to cover the costs of promotion and marketing. In practice, 12b-1 fees are usually used to reimburse the fund for commissions paid to brokers who sold the shares. In such instances, the 12b-1 fee takes the place of a *front-end load*. The fee is included in the expense ratio of funds and is therefore somewhat invisible to investors.

Value investor. Someone who seeks stocks that are considered undervalued according to some fundamental yardstick. This could be a stock that sells at a below-average *price-earnings ratio* or for less than the entire business might fetch on the private market.

Yield. The return earned by the income from an investment. For stocks, this would be dividend income over a year's time divided by the current share price. For bonds, it is the annual interest divided by the price. "Coupon yield" is the interest divided by the original price, or *par* value. "Current yield" is the interest income divided by the present price of the bond. "Yield to maturity" is the rate that takes into account the current yield and the difference between the purchase price and the face value, with the difference presumed to be paid in equal installments over the remaining life of the bond.

Zero-coupon bond. A bond that pays all of its interest at maturity. The accrued interest is built into the par value of the bond, which is issued at a deep discount to par to reflect the absence of ongoing interest payments. "Zeros" are very volatile and are suited either for risk-averse investors who want to speculate on lower interest rates or for long-term investors who want to ensure a definite payoff at a predetermined time in the future.